More
Time
for
Sex

HARRIET SCHECHTER
AND VICKI T. GIBBS

More Time for Sex

The Organizing Guide for Busy Couples

A DUTTON BOOK

DUTTON

Published by the Penguin Group
Penguin Books USA Inc., 375 Hudson Street, New York, New York 10014, U.S.A.
Penguin Books Ltd, 27 Wrights Lane, London W8 5TZ, England
Penguin Books Australia Ltd, Ringwood, Victoria, Australia
Penguin Books Canada Ltd, 10 Alcorn Avenue, Toronto, Ontario, Canada M4V 3B2
Penguin Books (N.Z.) Ltd, 182–190 Wairau Road, Auckland 10, New Zealand

Penguin Books Ltd, Registered Offices:
Harmondsworth, Middlesex, England

First published by Dutton, an imprint of Dutton Signet,
a division of Penguin Books USA Inc.
Distributed in Canada by McClelland & Stewart Inc.

First Printing, February, 1995
1   3   5   7   9   10   8   6   4   2

REGISTERED TRADEMARK—MARCA REGISTRADA

LIBRARY OF CONGRESS CATALOGING-IN-PUBLICATION DATA:

Schechter, Harriet.
More time for sex : the organizing guide for busy couples / Harriet Schechter and Vicki T. Gibbs.
p.   cm.
A Dutton book.
ISBN 0-525-93842-7
1. Married people—United States—Time management.   2. Sex—Planning.   3. Man-women
relationships—United States.   I. Gibbs, Vicki Townsend.   II. Title.
HQ536.S36   1995
640'.43—dc20   94-23171
                                                                                            CIP

Printed in the United States of America
Set in Bodoni Book

Designed by Steven N. Stathakis

*To Henry
and
to Jake*

I'm suggesting we call sex something else, and it should include everything from kissing to sitting close together.

—SHERE HITE

The *More Time for Sex* Philosophy:

Any time that is not spent on love is wasted.

Contents

PART TWO: The Top 20 Organizing and
Time Management Challenges Couples Face

Acknowledgments

We are grateful to everyone who helped make this book a reality:

Our heartfelt gratitude to Diane Gage for her invaluable insight and assistance and for introducing us to our wonderful agent, Toni Lopopolo, whose hard work and winning ways are deeply appreciated.

We thank Andrew Leranth for his helpful suggestions and ideas for our book proposal. Our warmest appreciation to Marcia Richardson for her inspired design recommendations and for always being a delight to work with.

We have been blessed with wise and caring advisors at Dutton and specifically wish to thank Elaine Koster for her vision; and our editors, Ed Stackler and Arnold Dolin, for their scrupulous efforts on our behalf. We could not have wished for a better team. In addition, we appreciate the cheerful assistance of Leah Bassoff.

Closer to home, we warmly thank Stuart Schechter for his legal assistance and advice, and our husbands for their editorial input as well as for being such good sports about their "appearances" in this book. A hug of gratitude to Judi Willkins and the Better Worlde Galleria bookstore staff for letting us hold our meetings and planning sessions there.

A huge thank you to all of the couples who participated in interviews for this book. We also greatly value and appreciate the encouragement, advice, suggestions, resources and moral support provided by authors Tana Fletcher, Wendy Haskett, Mike Hernacki, Paula Jhung and Eva Shaw.

From Harriet:

To Joanne and Don DiSesa for their invaluable help and support when I was starting The Miracle Worker Organizing Service and for their ongoing friendship.

I owe a debt of gratitude to my colleagues who have, at various times over the years, mentored, inspired and encouraged me, especially Mary Anne Lessley, Stephanie Culp, Susan Silver, Sharon Kristensen and Lisa Kanarek. Special thanks to all of my wonderful clients who honor me by inviting me into their private lives.

I want to acknowledge the businesses, acquaintances and angels of mercy who have helped to make my life more pleasant, especially during the long process of producing this book: Jane and Frank Reilly and the Postal Annex+ crew; Ramin Hooshmand and Reza Mansoor at Cal Copy; Kerry Stratford and C.J. at Printing Etc.; John Restivo, the Mobile Mechanic; Beth West and Gail Voels at the P.O.; Kevin Breach at The Company; Marty at Ken Gibbings Video Service; and the San Diego Learning Annex team.

I am indeed fortunate to have so many people in my life who truly wish me well and who know how to share happiness. To my friends who bring me joy in so many different ways at different times: Nazilla Alderson, Carolyn Coffman, Barbara Chronowski, Sharon Demere, Cynthia Lynn Douglass, Donna Duckett, Art Durson, T. Fleischer, Andrew Jay Gross, Linda Kao, Rachel Chinitz Lewine, Betty McKinstry, Sheryl North, Ruth Williams and Kelli Williamson. And to the memory of Mark Alfrets, whose friendship, advice and humor are irreplaceable.

And last but not least, to my fantastic family, whose ongoing love, support and wisdom have always nurtured and sustained me: My mother, Pauline, and my father, Bill, true organizational opposites and truly terrific individuals; my brother, Stuart, who introduced me to Henry and therefore made this book possible; my sister, Janet, who inspired and encouraged me to become an organizer; my brother-in-law, Stan, my amazing nephew, Louis, and my lovely new niece, Irene; and my father-in-law, Henry Sr. And to my darling husband, Henry, who knows how to lose almost everything except his temper and his patience.

From Vicki:

A personal thank you to Diane Gage for being such a great friend and inspiration, and for opening the first door. To Annie Steel who I never properly thanked for all she did for me.

Thank you now and always to my wonderful family—far-flung yet close-knit. To my extraordinary mother whose patience and open-mindedness I constantly strive to emulate. To my siblings and their mates for always believing in me: Jeanne Townsend and Fred Hornbeck, Karen and Ken Samcoe, Jackie and Jim Storm, Terri and Dan Ashley, and Steve and Maria Townsend. To my many nieces, nephews and great-nieces and nephews, who keep the love growing. A special thank you to my one-in-a-million mother-in-law Rubye Gibbs—she's always there when we need her. And to Aunt Florence—there will never be another like her.

To my good friends Kathy, Jan and Becky—friends for life. To my friend and fellow writer Sylvia Tiersten, who always wants the best for me; to Jessica for all the years of fun and friendship; and to Kathi George, a new friend who helped me through a tough time.

Lastly, a big thank you to Emily and Loren, the two best kids a mother could possibly have. Although you take up a great deal of my time, I wouldn't have it any other way. And of course, to Jake, my best friend, my number one cheerleader and the world's best reason for finding More Time!

Fore~~word~~ ^{play}

This book is for all those couples who wish they had more time for fun and romance. It was written with two objectives in mind:

1. To show you and your mate how to reduce the stress and conflict that often occur when two people share living quarters, especially if you have different organizational styles and standards
2. To demonstrate how both of you can create more time for each other by reducing some of the commonplace clutter and chaos that often plague busy couples in these hectic times

Although couples with children may derive some benefit from this book, the advice it contains is geared toward couples without children.

More Time for Sex contains real-life anecdotes and realistic advice distilled from a blend of the authors' personal and professional experience. Harriet Schechter is a speaker and organizing consultant who has worked with hundreds of couples—she is also part of an "odd couple," married to her organizational opposite. Vicki T. Gibbs, a writer, editor, and speaker, has been married for fourteen years to a man whose organizational style matches her own, but their busy schedules continue to challenge them to find ways of devoting more time to each other. The book is written in the first-person "voice" of Harriet Schechter.

If you and your mate can commit to regularly using even one of the hundreds of time-saving or stress-reducing tips and techniques found between the covers of this book, odds are the two of you will have more time to spend under your own covers.

Here's to less nagging and more nuzzling!

Harriet Schechter
Vicki T. Gibbs

PART ONE

Days of Whine
and Roses

More Time for Sex (and Other Things You'd Rather Be Doing): Tips, Tools and Techniques for Taming Time

*H*ow much time do you and your mate spend, in the course of a week ...

- Looking for misplaced things? (_____ minutes/hours)
- Arguing about household chores such as laundry, dishes, trash or yardwork? (_____ minutes/hours)
- Picking up after each other? (_____ minutes/hours)
- Making love? (_____ minutes/hours)

If you're like most couples, you're spending a lot less time enjoying that last category than you could be.

This book will show you how to change your habits so that you can devote more of your time to the delightful things you could be doing together. Imagine—instead of searching for your keys or

hunting for your mate's sunglasses every day, you could be ...
well, just fill in the blank.

TIME AND THE TV GENERATION

In many ways, our concept of time has been shaped by television.
In the compressed-time world of 30-minute sitcoms and 30-second
sound bites, there is rarely any depiction of such mundane, time-
consuming tasks as doing laundry, dishes, filing or bill-paying—the
types of things that pile up and create clutter and chaos in a household when there's "no time" to do them. Consequently, there is an
entire generation which seems to feel that these tasks shouldn't take
any time at all. If you and your mate fall into this category, watch
out! I have shocking news for you: Everything Takes Time—
especially the things that don't seem to take any time on TV.

Speaking of TV, studies have shown that's where most of our
missing time goes. TV-watching is one of the most insidious time
traps. Unless you actively enjoy passively watching TV with your
spouse, I recommend that you turn off the TV—and the lights. You
may find that you have more time for sex just by doing that. But
in case you don't, read on.

TIME IS MONEY—OR IS IT?

You've probably heard the expression "Time is money," attributed to
Benjamin Franklin (who, by the way, always seemed to have enough
time for hanky-panky no matter how busy he was—and he was
plenty busy). Most people don't
question that saying, but I think
it's time you did. The fact is, time
isn't money, or anything else for
that matter. Time is time, and
we're each allotted just 24 hours in
each day and seven days in each
week. That's all any of us gets—
period. You can get more money

> *"The average amount of time
> that the average American
> spends in the course of a life-
> time, looking for misplaced
> things, is one year."*
> — HARPER'S INDEX

(impossible as that sometimes seems) but you'll never have more than 168 hours in a week. So how you spend those hours is vitally important.

YOUR TIME BUDGET

Even though your time isn't money, if you try to budget it as though it were dollars, you'll see whether you're wasting it or spending it wisely. The Budget-Time Worksheet on the next page is designed to help you and your mate do this. So, pick up a pencil and get started.

Use the first form (page 6) to see how you're currently spending your time (and be honest!).

Then, use the form on page 7 to create an ideally balanced time budget—and try to be realistic. For example, don't cut your sleep time down to two hours just so you can have more time for . . . other things.

TO WASTE OR NOT TO WASTE

When you're done, take a few minutes to glance over your completed Budget-Time Worksheet. You'll probably quickly spot the category you should reduce or eliminate. By learning to understand how to organize your time and space more effectively, you'll be able to not only virtually eliminate the "Wasted Time" slot, but also reduce the time spent on household chores and errands as well. You can then use that time to . . . do whatever you and your partner decide to do.

When Vicki first married, she was pretty good at getting places on time. (Okay, she was fairly good . . . okay, she was fair.) But she slowly seemed to get later and later. In an effort to remedy the situation, her husband Jake secretly set her watch and all the clocks in the house

> *"Many people take no care of their money till they come nearly to the end of it, and others do just the same with their time."*
>
> — *GOETHE*

BUDGET-TIME WORKSHEET
THE WAY IT IS NOW

WEEKLY FUND OF HOURS   168

Sleep Time (_____ × 7)   – _____

Personal Time (_____ × 7)
(bathroom, dressing, etc.)   – _____

Eating Time (_____ × 7)   – _____

Couple Time (_____)
(sex, cuddling, conversations)   – _____

Exercise/Sports (_____)   – _____

Household Chores Time (_____)   – _____

Errand Time (_____)
(banking, shopping, P. O., etc.)   – _____

Family Time (_____)
(calls, visits, correspondence, etc.)   – _____

Friend Time (_____)
(calls, visits, correspondence, etc.)   – _____

Entertainment Time (_____)
(movies, theatre, TV, reading books, magazines,
newspapers)   – _____

Charity Time (_____)
(nonprofit organizations, etc.)   – _____

Professional Activity Time (_____)
(business reading, networking groups, etc.)   – _____

Work Time (_____)   – _____

Paperwork & Planning Time (_____)   – _____

Gap Time (_____)
(travel/commute time, waiting time)   – _____

Wasted Time (_____)
(looking for misplaced things, etc.)   – _____

REMAINDER   0 hours

YOUR IDEAL WEEK

WEEKLY FUND OF HOURS   168

Sleep Time (_____ × 7)   – _____

Personal Time (_____ × 7)
(bathroom, dressing, etc.)   – _____

Eating Time (_____ × 7)   – _____

Couple Time (_____)
(sex, cuddling, conversations)   – _____

Exercise/Sports (_____)   – _____

Household Chores Time (_____)   – _____

Errand Time (_____)
(banking, shopping, P. O., etc.)   – _____

Family Time (_____)
(calls, visits, correspondence, etc.)   – _____

Friend Time (_____)
(calls, visits, correspondence, etc.)   – _____

Entertainment Time (_____)
(movies, theatre, TV, reading books, magazines,
newspapers)   – _____

Charity Time (_____)
(nonprofit organizations, etc.)   – _____

Professional Activity Time (_____)
(business reading, networking groups, etc.)   – _____

Work Time (_____)   – _____

Paperwork & Planning Time (_____)   – _____

Gap Time (_____)
(travel/commute time, waiting time)   – _____

Wasted Time (_____)
(looking for misplaced things, etc.)   – _____

REMAINDER   0 hours

ahead ten minutes. It took her two months to realize what he had done, but by that time she was used to being almost on time for appointments again, so she decided to keep her watch fast to help her be prompt. And Jake got a kiss, instead of a kick.

THE IMPORTANCE OF "WHITE SPACE"

People who design ads for newspapers and magazines know the value of "white space." An effective ad generally has a good balance between white space (unfilled area) and ad copy/graphics. If an advertisement is cluttered with too many words or images, it usually won't work—readers will skip right over it.

Take a look at your calendar or time management system. Does it look like a poorly designed ad, with too many words and not enough white space? If you and your mate don't regularly block out white space in your schedules, you may find that you get over-committed—and not to each other. White space (or Gap Time on your Budget-Time Worksheet) functions as a sort of shock-absorber for schedule bumps such as heavy traffic, waiting in line or in doctors' offices and other unforeseen but inevitable circumstances. And, if occasionally things go smoothly and you don't run into any time glitches, you can use that white space to stop and smell the roses—and maybe pick some for your spouse.

TAKE TIME TO MAKE TIME

Set aside time with your mate each week to look at each other's schedules so you can try to plan a weekly date together. Yes, it does take time to plan, and sometimes things won't work out and one of you will need to be late or reschedule; but if you make a habit of it, by and large you'll find that the rewards far outweigh the perceived inconvenience. Be sure to pencil in your weekly date several weeks ahead of time.

TWO TYPES OF TIME

When it comes to reorganizing your time and space it's helpful to think in terms of two types of time: Project Time and Maintenance Time. Project Time is the hours you spend on projects such as setting up a filing system or cleaning out the garage; repairing or creating things utilizes Project Time. Maintenance Time is the time you spend when you do any of the following types of ongoing chores:

Washing dishes	Paying bills
Doing laundry	Filing
Grocery shopping	Checking car fluids
Housecleaning	Washing car
Cooking	Walking dog/cleaning litterbox
Making beds	Watering
Mowing lawn	Taking out trash
Weeding	Running errands

Let's face it—most of what we do is maintenance! In fact, I have a saying—"Life is 5 percent joy, 5 percent grief, and 90 percent maintenance." And unless you understand and accept this concept, you'll be doomed to a life of wondering why things aren't the way you thought they were supposed to be.

At the risk of sounding sexist, generally speaking, women seem to grasp this concept more easily than men, at least in my highly biased experience. If you don't believe it, ask the elves.

THE ELVES PHENOMENON

It has not gone unnoticed by millions of people (mostly women) that millions of other people (mostly men) seem to believe in elves—specifically, in those elves who magically fill drawers with clean, folded laundry; who replace office supplies in the twinkling

> "Life is 5 percent joy, 5 percent grief and 90 percent mainte-nance."
>
> — HARRIET SCHECHTER

of an eye; who put things back in place so that they can be mis-placed over and over again . . . you get the idea. (In one of my workshops, when I described the Elves Phenomenon, a woman raised her hand and said how re-lieved she was to hear that her husband wasn't the only one who, as she put it, "seems to think that there are a hundred little elves running around behind him doing his bidding and picking up after him as he tears through the house.")

I have disappointing news: THERE ARE NO ELVES! At least not in this sense of the word. This fact was proven rather harshly to a woman I knew. Years ago, when she was very young and newly married, she would throw all dirty clothes and linens into a closet, which was what she had done when she lived at her parents' home. She then expected the laundry to be magically taken care of. Eventually, she and her husband ran out of clean clothes. They were very puzzled until the truth finally dawned: They had moved away from the elves! (And no, this woman wasn't Vicki or me, in case you're wondering.)

It is crucial to a healthy household relationship that both members of a couple understand this point: Each of you is respon-sible for certain maintenance tasks on an ongoing basis. Unless you take the time early on in your couplehood to define household maintenance tasks and figure out who is responsible for what, you're in for years of disagreements and disappointments (and probably a lot less sex than you'd have if you weren't so busy ar-guing about whose turn it is to take out the trash).

> "Well-arranged time is a good sign of a well-arranged mind."
>
> — FORTUNE COOKIE

I've identified five sequen-tial steps toward creating and maintaining an equitable and manageable division of household chores. First, however, it's impor-tant that both of you understand and accept the concept of "90 percent maintenance." If one partner refuses to do his or her fair share of maintenance, and if the other partner perceives this as a problem, consider the following options:

- Paying a third party to do the chores that one partner refuses to do.
- Having that partner pay you to do those chores.
- You do them for "free" in exchange for the right to nag and complain ceaselessly.

Couples counseling is also a valid option for certain situations.

FIVE STEPS TO SHARING HOUSEHOLD CHORES

1. DEFINE MAINTENANCE TASKS
2. AGREE ON RESPONSIBILITIES

I've already done Step #2 for you. (At no extra charge, too!) The checklist on pages 12 to 13 is fairly thorough. Some of the tasks, such as pet care or gardening chores, may not apply to your life-style; just cross out those that aren't a match, and add any others not listed in the spaces provided at the end.

Before moving to Step #3, you'll need to have two other things in hand: your spouse or "significant other," and a pencil. Sit down together and divide up the tasks listed below by putting your initials in the blanks next to tasks that you don't mind doing regularly, and have your mate do the same. In some cases, you may prefer to alternate certain tasks from week to week or day to day; in those instances, pencil in both sets of initials.

If you've been together for several years and are trying to reassign responsibilities, you may first use the checklist to designate which chores you each are currently doing and then do a new checklist assigning the chores the way you would like them to be done.

HOUSEHOLD MAINTENANCE CHECKLIST
FOR COUPLES

Kitchen
__ Meal planning
__ Grocery shopping
__ Putting away groceries
__ Cooking
__ Setting & clearing table
__ Washing dishes/loading dishwasher
__ Drying dishes/unloading dishwasher
__ Putting away dishes

Trash/Recycling
__ Gathering trash inside house to put in outside cans
__ Putting out trash cans for pick up
__ Putting recycling at curb (if you have this service)
__ Loading recycling in car to take to center
__ Taking recycling to recycling center

Bedrooms
__ Making bed
__ Changing bedding

Laundry
__ Gathering & sorting laundry
__ Loading washing machine/dryer
__ Folding clean laundry
__ Ironing/steaming
__ Putting away clean laundry

Cleaning
__ Picking up clutter
__ Dusting
__ Cleaning bathroom(s)
__ Vacuuming
__ Washing windows
__ Cleaning floors

Errands
__ Dropping off/picking up dry cleaning
__ Banking errands

___ Hardware store
___ Returning library books

Home Office
___ Sorting/processing incoming mail
___ Paying bills
___ Filing/handling household paperwork
___ Answering correspondence/sending thank-yous
___ Money maintenance (e.g., balancing checkbook, budgeting, tracking investments)

Outside/Landscape
___ Mowing lawn
___ Weeding
___ Watering/fertilizing

Pets
___ Walking dog
___ Washing/grooming pet(s)
___ Feeding pets
___ Trips to vet
___ Scooping poop/emptying litterbox/cleaning aquarium

Vehicle Maintenance
___ Checking/replacing tires
___ Taking cars for tune-ups
___ Checking/replacing fluids
___ Washing/waxing

Seasonal Chores
___ Shopping for gifts
___ Writing thank-yous
___ Wrapping gifts
___ Entertainment planning/follow-through

Other

_____

_____

_____

3. DEFINE STANDARDS

This step can be tricky because it is highly subjective and usually will involve compromise. It can also cause friction, so be prepared. What is clean or neat to one person may be unacceptable to the other half of a couple. For example, your spouse may find it sufficient to stuff clean laundry into a drawer any which way, while you are constitutionally incapable of putting underwear away without folding it perfectly.

Although Doug and Becky are not married and they maintain separate residences, they spend a great deal of time at her beautifully furnished, well-maintained three-bedroom home. Therefore, Doug thinks it's only fair that he do his share of the cleaning. After many years of a previous marriage and a year or so on his own, Doug says, "I thought I knew how to clean." But he learned otherwise when he tried to help Becky clean. In the kitchen, for example, when he would clean up, she would come along behind him and clean it again. It was the same with the bathroom. He says, "I've cleaned bathrooms. I went to college. I know you get out the Comet . . ." But she wants it done her way, so he has learned to stand back and let her do it.

A difference in standards can cause problems. After some rocky starts, Becky and Doug were able to work it out. Basically, he cooks and takes care of the yard, but she does most of the cleaning. And that's okay with her, because then she knows it will be done to her satisfaction.

When you and your mate divide up chores and define standards, be certain that you make choices you can live with. It's one thing to be agreeable, but don't accept something you truly don't feel is right just to keep the peace. There's got to be compromise on both sides. If you both adamantly detest cleaning out the cat's litterbox, but you can't live without feline companionship, then take turns doing the chore

> "Housecleaning and sex are alike in that people always lie about how often they do them."
> — PAULA JHUNG

so that one person isn't stuck feeling resentful at having to do it all the time.

To properly define standards, you'll need to set aside about an hour of uninterrupted time with your mate to do a "walk-through" of your home together. Bring your Household Maintenance Checklist (pages 12 to 13) and a ruled pad and pencil with you. Some points you may need to clarify with each other might include:

- What is a mutually acceptable standard of "clean" for dishes and other food-related utensils and for bathrooms and kitchens?
- When is it okay to leave out such items as shaving equipment, hairbrushes and cosmetics, and when isn't it? Should clothing always be put away after wearing or can it be left draped over chairs and door knobs?
- Who is responsible for replenishing supplies such as toilet paper, soap and paper towels?
- Where should various shared items be kept?
- Why is it important to put away clothes instead of leaving them in the dryer?

This is just a short list to start you thinking. More issues may come to mind during your tour, but this should get you started.

Let's take a hypothetical couple, Tom and Brenda, through a tour of their home to help them define standards. First stop is the kitchen. For Tom, the kitchen is clean if the dishes are washed, rinsed, and in the drainer. Brenda, however, believes that all countertops and the dining table should also be wiped clean of crumbs and spills and the area should be generally picked up. After some discussion, Tom agrees that Brenda is probably right and on nights that he cleans the kitchen he will do a more complete job. (Obviously this is hypothetical!)

Next stop is the bathroom. When it comes to getting ready in the mornings, Tom likes to have the counter area cleared and

"To be happy at home is the ultimate result of all ambition, the end to which every enterprise and labour tends."
— SAMUEL JOHNSON

clean. Brenda, on the other hand, likes to keep her cleansing creams, lotions and perfumes on the counter. This bothers Tom, who feels that her personal items are encroaching on mutual space. After more discussion, Brenda agrees to organize her drawers and cabinets in such a way that she won't find it necessary to keep things out on the counter.

Hot Tip: Use small plastic utility baskets that fit in drawers and on shelves to group various cosmetics and toiletry items. This will save time when taking things out or putting them back.

They both agree that keeping the counters, bathtub and toilet bowl sparkling clean will make for a nicer bathroom.

When it comes to replacing toilet paper, their rule is: He who uses the last sheet replaces the roll. They always keep a spare roll or two close at hand. (Have you ever discussed with your mate about which way to put the paper on the roll? Should it roll from the top or from underneath? For some couples, this can be a matter of utmost importance.)

Brenda and Tom had no disagreement about clothes coming out of the dryer as soon as they are dry. They both are professionals and want to look crisp and fresh. Some people don't feel this way. One couple I worked with only took clothes out of the dryer as they needed to wear them. When the dryer was empty it was time to run another load.

4. ALLOCATE TIME

A key time management concept that most people neglect is scheduling appointments with themselves—not just with other people—so that they can get things done. Unless you and your mate can get in the habit of doing this, it will be extremely difficult to "find" the time to do either maintenance or projects. Utilizing

"Anyone can do any amount of work provided it isn't the work he is supposed to be doing at the moment."

— *ROBERT BENCHLEY*

a time management system such as Day-Timer or DayRunner (and there are dozens more) will assist you with this process.

A good time management system (also known as an activity management system, personal planner or organizer) should do the following:

- It should allow you to schedule blocks of time for appointments with yourself as well as appointments with others. This will help you to break down large projects into manageable segments.

- It should provide a place for you to note and subsequently schedule all things to be done, whether it's a note about taking clothes to the dry cleaner or preparing research for a business project. Remember—a "to do" list without a timeline is of limited value.

- It should serve as a "memory bank" for you—a place to keep information such as important phone numbers and other things you may need to refer to, so you don't have to clutter your mind with details. A good system remembers things for you, freeing you to concentrate on creative rather than mundane thoughts. (It's said that Einstein chose not to memorize his own telephone number, since he knew where he could look it up—he didn't want to waste his brain cells!)

- It should give you a sense of being in control of your time, instead of vice versa. If your time management system is working for you, you will rarely—if ever—have that nagging feeling that you've forgotten something you need to do.

5. SET UP A "REWARDS PROGRAM" TO PROVIDE INCENTIVES

Remember the "5 percent joy, 5 percent grief, 90 percent maintenance" equation? Well, if you can learn how to make maintenance tasks more enjoyable, you'll increase your quota of joy. One way to do this is to set up a *rewards program* to provide incentives for accomplishing routine household chores. (This may seem silly at first, but then so do many games that actually turn out to be fun.) The rewards need not cost anything; the worksheet which follows should give you some ideas for the types of things that could constitute rewards.

HOW TO SET UP A REWARDS PROGRAM

"Virtue is its own reward." Perhaps—but sometimes we need other forms of motivation. Plan to treat yourself to something special each time you manage to complete a task you've previously put off doing, or when you finish part (or all) of a project.

On the next page are Rewards Categories, with spaces for you to fill in specific kinds of rewards that might appeal to you and your mate. The rewards should be appropriate to your budget and realistic in terms of your lifestyle and available time.

REWARDS IDEAS LIST

Places to Go
Ideas:
Art Galleries
Beaches/Scenic Drive
Bookstores
Museums
Parks
Window Shopping

_____

_____

_____

Arts/Entertainment
Ideas:
Comedy
Concerts
Dance
Movies
TV
Video

_____

_____

_____

To Read/Hear
Ideas:
Books
CDs/Tapes/Albums
Lectures/Classes
Magazines

_____

_____

_____

Gifts
Ideas:
Flowers
Cookies
Wine
Sexy underwear

_____

_____

_____

Romance
With each other:
Candlelight dinner
Bubblebath
Hot Tub
Massage

Miscellaneous
You name it:

_____   _____

_____   _____

_____   _____

 TIMELY TIPS

- Less stuff = more time. Learn the importance of getting rid of stuff. You can always get more stuff, but you can never get more time.

- Make use of a ticking timer for all sorts of tasks. The ticking will remind you that time is passing and you'll be less likely to get distracted or waste that time. You can even get a ticking timer on a cord (see page 183) to wear around your neck when you take a walk just to keep you focused on your goal of getting some exercise, not just meandering down the street.

- Set up your household so that things you need are close to where they are used. This will save not only time but also your energy—you'll take fewer wasted steps.

- Screen your calls with an answering machine. That way the phone doesn't rule you. Many times people use phone calls as an excuse to get sidetracked from what they are supposed to be doing.

- Take five minutes at the end of each day to take stock of the day just past and to organize tomorrow. Use a pencil instead of a pen for more flexibility.

2

Yours, Mine and Ours: Blending Two Separate Lives—and Households—Into One

*S*haring your life with the one you love can bring joy and happiness, love and passion. It can mean romantic nights in front of a fire and dinners for two by candlelight. On the other hand, it can mean fights over who was supposed to pick up the wine and candles and who left the damp sheets mildewing in the washing machine.

Contrary to what Hollywood would have us believe, life as a couple is not always romance and roses. And today more than ever, just getting through the everyday stresses and strains of working and maintaining a household can drain a couple so that they have little energy or interest left for the romantic and fun parts of life— the parts that probably brought them together in the first place.

But don't despair. It is possible to have busy, fulfilling lives at work, keep a clean, well-managed home, and still have time left for leisurely evening pillow talk or more aerobic romps, if that's your style. It takes planning and follow-through—but it's worth it.

ALL THAT STUFF

Most people come to a relationship with hopes and dreams and plans for the future. They also bring with them, however, all their stuff, not to mention years and years worth of habits and attitudes. Trying to blend all this stuff and these habits and attitudes with someone else's stuff, habits and attitudes can be a nightmare.

First, there's all that stuff. Today, many people are waiting longer to get married or live together. Couples are anxious to get their individual careers going strong before they commit to a relationship. That can translate into almost a decade of single life in some cases. Consequently, by the time they are ready to marry or cohabit, these folks have each collected a household of furniture, linens, books, stereo equipment, and kitchen appliances. Likewise, they may each have a car, a condo, a washer and dryer, and numerous adult toys, like snow skis, ski boats, dune buggies and more. Then, if they have a large wedding, they'll end up with still more stuff.

That's great, you might say. Better than starting with nothing. Perhaps. But if both members of a couple come to the relationship with this much "stuff," how is it all going to fit? And what if each has a much-loved house, condo or apartment—where will they live? And who will give up some of his or her precious possessions so that two full households can be crammed into one?

When Vicki married at the age of 29, it took several weeks for her and Jake to squeeze everything from her fully furnished two-bedroom house into his more-than-fully furnished two-bedroom condo. Working together, they found places for two popcorn poppers pers, two blenders, two juicers, and myriad towels, washcloths, sheets and blankets. They also discovered that, thanks to economy-minded shopping, they were now the proud owners of five gallons of window cleaner, fifteen household cleaning brushes, and a two-year supply of bathroom cleaner.

> "We tend to confuse the good life with a life of goods."
> — SIMON SCHAMA

HABITS AND ATTITUDES

Then there are all those habits. You may have spent the last 15 years falling asleep to the soothing sounds of classical music played softly on a bedside radio, while your mate, on the other hand, can't possibly slip into slumber without the squawking of a bedside police scanner reporting every break-in, robbery and murder in the vicinity. He may keep his half of the closet perfectly organized with nary a pair of trousers out of place. You, however, need at least ten minutes each morning to dig through all five of your bureau drawers to find a pair of pantyhose without a runner from heel to thigh.

Worse than bad habits, and harder to change, are attitudes. Each member of a couple comes to the relationship with certain well-entrenched attitudes about how a household should be set up and maintained. One person might make it a regular practice to each month toss out old newspapers and magazines and bundle up a box of giveaways for the Salvation Army. The other partner, however, might feel it's essential to keep every issue of *National Geographic* that's ever received, just in case it's ever needed for researching Indians from the jungles of Brazil or learning about the rivers of Asia.

One gentleman Vicki knows has kept every single textbook he's ever been issued . . . just in case he ever needs to get to that information again. He's apparently never heard about public libraries. And because he now has two master's degrees and is close to a doctorate, his poor wife is looking into having a library of their own built into a spare corner to house all these dusty tomes.

> *"If everyone keeps stacking* National Geographics *in garages and attics instead of throwing them away, the magazine's weight will sink the continent 100 feet some time soon and we will all be inundated by the oceans."*
>
> — *JOURNAL OF IRREPRODUCIBLE RESULTS*

Most of us exhibit one of three basic attitudes. First, there's the attitude of acquisition. People with this outlook believe they must own everything, whether or not they have space for it or a real need for it. They keep several years worth of back issues of all the magazines they subscribe to. Their shelves are stocked with every appliance known to humankind. And often there is only a tiny three-foot path through their garage because of all the excess "stuff" that gets dumped out there.

If you have this attitude, you need to realize that it may result in negative consequences. It will be more difficult to maintain organization because you must constantly find new places to file and store the things you are bringing in.

Then there are people who have the opposite attitude. They are constantly getting rid of things. They delight in keeping the local thrift shops stocked with near-new clothing and shoes, not to mention books, appliances, and knickknacks.

And finally, there are those who are able to strike a nice balance between what comes in and what goes out. Not keeping around unnecessary items and old copies of magazines and newspapers, they manage to live relatively uncluttered lives with time and space to spare.

Attitudes, habits and stuff . . . all things that can be changed, if both people agree that doing so would be beneficial for them individually and as a couple.

A LITTLE RESPECT

Creating more time for sex by being better organized sounds like a good idea. But, if that organization is achieved by one partner nagging and browbeating the other about his or her habits, there's not likely to be much interest in romance even when there is time for it. That's why acceptance and respect are essential elements when it comes to blending two lives.

A couple can start by identifying and respecting each other's organizational styles. Just be-

> *"The only time a woman really succeeds in changing a man is when he is a baby."*
> — *NATALIE WOOD*

> *"The concept of two people living together without serious dispute suggests a lack of spirit to be admired only in sheep."*
> — A. P. HERBERT

cause your spouse doesn't think it's necessary to make the bed the moment it's vacated, and maybe even lets it go unmade all day now and then, doesn't make him or her a bad person. Always remember, what bothers you is the behavior, not the person. Rather than thinking of your mate as messy, consider that maybe he or she has a more "relaxed" style than you do—it's not something that must be changed or conquered.

By the time most of us marry, our habits are pretty well ingrained. We do things a certain way, and we're comfortable with that style. To maintain peace in the family when partners have two different styles of housekeeping and maintenance, it's important to remember that people will not change their habits unless they want to. Plus, it's unlikely they will change at all unless they see specific benefits to changing.

If some of your mate's habits truly make you crazy, you need to sit down and discuss them with him or her. Begin by realizing that your way of doing things is not inherently the right way. In fact, there are numerous ways of doing the same thing and none of them is right or wrong.

Say, for example, your spouse has a habit of piling mail, magazines, newspapers, and all other types of incoming papers in several big piles around the kitchen and family room. If this method has caused you to lose important papers or maybe has cost you finance charges on bills paid late, you should probably discuss the possibility of your mate changing this particular habit.

First, pick a calm time to have the discussion. Don't bring it up right after you discover the vehicle registration fees you thought he paid last month are now overdue and are going to cost an additional $80.00. Wait until you've calmed down and can talk to him without placing blame. Then, discuss the advantages and disadvantages of the behavior. What would be the rewards if he were

to change his style of piling everything together? What can you
do to help him change this habit?
What will be the disadvantages if
he continues to operate in this
manner? (Bodily harm is not a
recommended option.)

*"Some of us are like wheel-
barrows—only useful when
pushed, and very easily upset."*
— JACK HERBERT

Remember, when having these discussions, always be willing
to compromise. Say you're a well-organized man who is married to
a woman who has no neatness genes in her DNA string at all. Does
that make her a bad person? No. It just means you'll have to be
willing to compromise a little to insure happiness . . . but so will
she. You may think it's essential that clean clothes be neatly folded
and placed in stacks in the drawer, rather than left in the laundry
basket to be retrieved as needed. That's great, in theory, but you
may have to settle for dumped from the laundry basket into the
drawer . . . to be retrieved as needed.

A SPACE OF ONE'S OWN

In this country, many of us are blessed with a place to live that not
only keeps us warm and dry, but also serves as a haven from the
everyday stresses and strains of life—a place to take off our shoes,
put up our feet and be ourselves. (Of course, where you drop those
shoes when you take them off might be a subject of discussion).
But, when we share our personal haven with another human being,
we must always keep that person's likes and dislikes in mind while
still trying to be ourselves and relax. This can be a real challenge
when one partner is tidy and the other isn't. That's why it's important to always be sure each member of the couple has a
space of his or her own. It's not necessary that each person have
his or her own room, although if you can afford the space to do
this, enjoy it. Just a small area of the house or apartment which is
strictly for you and you alone, to be kept in whatever shape you
wish to keep it, can provide each of you with a sense of well-being.

If your mate is a "messy" and his space happens to be the

> "Light is the task when many
> share the toil."
>   — HOMER

corner of your well-maintained master bedroom, you might want to purchase a decorative screen to place between you and what you might consider an eyesore. But by all means, let your mate keep that space in whatever state he chooses. Otherwise, you lose the value of his having a space to do with as he pleases.

Doug, whom we met in Chapter One, claims that "Clutter" is probably his middle name. Becky, his partner, agrees. But that didn't mean she was happy about picking up after him everywhere he went. They finally hit upon the perfect solution. They designated a chair as his own personal space. He could pile on it to his heart's content—and he does. He says, "It's kind of like a shrine." And Becky just ignores it.

They also decided it would make sense for him to have his own desk. Again, though he doesn't keep it the way she would, she respects his right to his space.

According to Doug, "It was one of the most important things we've done to keep this relationship alive. She gave me my own space in her house and I don't have to change for her or try to change her to be like me."

Remember too, if you are the tidy one, you also need a space to call your own, where you can keep things neatly stacked and categorized—a place where mess and disorganization never raise their ugly heads.

Sometimes, the more meticulous half of a couple will keep his or her space and all the mutual spaces so organized and inviting that the messy half is drawn to these places to work and relax. Often, the messier one will gradually infringe on these spaces by starting to pile his or her stuff there when the neater one isn't looking.

I found this to be the case when my husband, Henry, who has his own personal space (affectionately nicknamed "The Pit"), began to bring his Rolodex into the master bedroom to make business calls. It was, not surprisingly, a much more pleasant place to make phone calls than in The Pit. Gradually, other pieces of detritus from The Pit began to slither their way into the bedroom. First a "While You Were Out" form or two appeared on the bedspread. Then business cards with cryptic messages scribbled on them began to show up on the bedside table.

Rather than ranting or raving about constantly having to return the Rolodex to The Pit, I adapted. (Okay. Maybe I did rant and rave a little at first.) Here's what I did: First I set up a little hideaway spot for the Rolodex, and then purchased a small rolling wastebasket that fits perfectly under the bedside table. This holds telephone message books, pens, pencils and anything else that might stray down the hall.

HOW "THE PIT" WAS CREATED

I'm fond of telling people that it took me four years to decide that I could, in fact, marry Henry and live happily with him in spite of the fact that he was incredibly disorganized. (In my opinion, it's his only flaw—almost.) I knew he probably was never going to change, which meant that I was the one who would have to do most of the adapting. (Of course there are still times when I blow up at Henry for, say, dropping his dirty clothes on the floor right next to his hamper.)

After marrying Henry, the first thing I did was "excavate" his house. It was a perfectly nice three-bedroom house that he and two tenant roommates ("boarders" dignifies them unnecessarily) had probably never cleaned. It was stuffed with everything from mounds of old newspapers to various unidentifiable rusting parts and tools. Once it was cleared out—with a certain percentage of the mysterious items stashed in the garage and storage shed—it was ready for some minor remodeling; new carpet and flooring, fresh paint and blinds, etc.

There was one small room, however, which was spared. Early on in the excavating and remodeling process, I noticed that Henry seemed especially fond of the disaster that had been his old bedroom. So I asked him if he wanted me to help him organize it and get it redone—or leave it alone. Much to my chagrin, he told me, "This is the only room that still feels like me—so it's okay if you leave it alone." Thus was born "The Pit," my fond nickname for Henry's space of his own.

RULES OF THE PIT

Once I recognized that Henry needed a space of his own, I began to see that The Pit could actually make my life easier by providing a drop-off point for any clutter that Henry might leave around the house. But in order for The Pit to work well for both of us, we had to establish some Pit rules:

1. No matter how messy it gets, Harriet does not attempt to clean up or organize anything in The Pit without Henry's permission and presence. (The exception: She will infiltrate for any clothes he accidentally leaves in The Pit.)
2. Nothing Henry leaves around the house gets tossed without his permission, but within 24 hours Harriet will transfer it to The Pit (usually the floor just inside the door, since that's the only clear surface).
3. The door to The Pit will be kept closed most of the time.

Early on in our marriage, I decided to accept that having a well-organized, neat, clean home was important to me—but not to Henry. What this means is that, since Henry doesn't really care how the inside of the house looks, it's completely unrealistic to expect him to. No amount of arguing, cajoling, pleading or threatening will ever effect more than a temporary change in Henry's (or any mate's) behavior. But since he's extremely easygoing and good-natured and therefore very easy to live with overall, I decided that I'd rather pick up after him than harass him continu-

WIRE SERVICE REPORT—A woman in La Verne, California, told police her ex-boyfriend broke into her apartment and forced her, at gunpoint, to clean the place up during a three-hour ordeal.

ously, especially because now I can just dump everything in The Pit. (Instead I harass him just occasionally.)

While I don't really mind picking up after Henry (most of the time, anyway) it is important to me to feel that he appreciates what I do. That's why we came up with a weekly ritual—every Monday he brings me a big bouquet of flowers. It's a relatively inexpensive gesture which nevertheless takes time and effort and which, most importantly, makes me happy.

Acknowledgment goes both ways: I make a point of complimenting Henry whenever I see him make an effort to pick up after himself. And slowly but surely he has gotten in the habit of hanging up his clothes and filing some of his papers—things he never did before.

Although it does take time initially to discover—and work with—each other's habits, styles and needs, it will save you time in the long run. And I'll bet that you and your love can think of some pleasant ways to spend that surplus time.

What if both of you have trouble staying organized and keeping your household in order? Well, all of the previously described suggestions still apply—only it may be tougher for an "organizationally impaired" couple to implement them without some outside assistance, such as a professional organizer or counselor.

The "10 Basic Rules for Getting and Staying Organized" (on the next page) may provide a focus.

10 BASIC RULES FOR GETTING & STAYING ORGANIZED

1. *Take time to make time:* Learn to regularly set aside uninterrupted time for accomplishing tasks such as filing, correspondence, bill-paying, putting things away, etc. A ticking timer can help keep you on track.

2. *Plan your week:* At the end of each week, sit down with your calendar and your "to do" lists and plan the next week. Allocate time for the things you want to accomplish; don't overbook yourself; and use an erasable pen or pencil so you can adapt your plan to accommodate changes.

3. *Create a workspace:* Set up an area that's comfortable for you to sit and work on projects or maintenance work (such as those tasks described in #1).

4. *Categorize:* Put like things together, and group like tasks together to save time.

5. *Practice making decisions:* Exercise your decision-making muscles on a regular basis instead of putting things aside "till later." Remember—very few decisions are irrevocable, so don't be afraid to make them. Make the decision—and move on!

6. *Make it easy:* Put things in convenient places; don't just put supplies where they fit—put them close to where they'll be used. Get rid of things that don't work well and replace them with products and procedures that are easy to maintain and a pleasure to use.

7. *Put things back:* If you do #6, this will be easier.

8. *Make sure a surface is clear* . . . before you put something down on it "just for now"—so you don't hide what's underneath and then lose time (and sanity) looking for things later.

9. *Establish an "In/Out Inventory Rule":* For each item (such as books, clothes, supplies) that comes into your home or office, another item of equal size should go out (to charity, trash, etc.).

10. *Reward yourself for accomplishing what you set out to do:* Make sure you have something to look forward to, to motivate yourself to get certain tasks done. Whether it's "quiet time" alone with a book or magazine, an outing with a friend, or another special treat . . . you may want to keep a list or file of "Fun Things To Do" so you always have ideas handy for your rewards; see Rewards Ideas List, page 18.

TIMELY TIPS

- Budget your money so that you can somehow manage to pay a cleaning service to clean your home every other week. This type of service is usually surprisingly affordable. Unless you're really broke, you should be able to find a way to do it, even if it means cutting down on magazine subscriptions or beer or some other luxury you think you can't live without. Unless you and/or your mate really enjoys cleaning toilets and vacuuming and dusting and all the related maintenance, I urge you to explore this option. "Cleaning up before the maid comes"—which should mean just putting things away so that surfaces are clear, not actually cleaning—will help insure that your place stays reasonably neat.

- Keep frequently used supplies handy in each room. Things like scissors, pen/pencil, notepaper, tape, Post-its, letter opener, calculator, etc., can be assembled in a small basket or other suitable container and placed discreetly throughout your home. Not only will these items be "right there" when you need them (thereby saving you the time of going into another room to get them) but it will be much easier for both of you to put things back when you're done using them—eliminating the common problem of "whoever used it last, forgot to put it back."

- If you have an argument about who put what where and who lost which what, don't forget to kiss and make up before bedtime. "Don't go to bed mad" is still good advice!

- Create an end-of-the-day daily ritual together. A five-minute foot massage can do wonders for your tired mate's tootsies; in turn, you may enjoy a backrub while discussing your day. Or perhaps you'd prefer just jumping in the hot tub together (or the shower, if that's what's available); or even just stretching out on the sofa for a cuddle and a chat. Mutually enjoyable moments like these give you something to look forward to at the end of each day. Such daily rituals also help to strengthen your relationship by giving you a regular time to unwind together and talk about what's on your mind. An added bonus: it doesn't cost a penny!

- Take time to say "I love you" at least daily to each other. Even though actions often speak louder than words, words are important, too.

- Spontaneous gestures of love and appreciation help to keep daily rituals from becoming mundane and predictable. Surprise your mate periodically with something different—a new massage oil, a relaxation tape, a cozy pair of slippersocks. It needn't cost much; the important thing is that you keep his or her tastes in mind.

3

Man & Wife, Inc.: The Business of Running a Household

*R*unning a household is somewhat like running a small business. Like all companies, couples have to deal with incoming and outgoing mail, which includes bills and correspondence; phone calls to be made and phone messages to be taken; budgeting, banking and other financial procedures; and, of course, filing.

To save time and reduce potential misunderstandings and frustration, it's wise to set up simple, flexible, growth-oriented systems that both mates can understand and operate with a minimum of effort. The systems described in this chapter are fairly easy to establish and maintain, but be sure to discuss with your spouse which of you will be responsible for handling the various maintenance tasks regularly. Before I get into those systems, let's talk about setting up a home office.

THE IMPORTANCE OF HAVING A HOME OFFICE

Virtually every type of company needs an office in which to conduct business, and a household is no exception. Whether you and your spouse share a palatial mansion or a tiny apartment, setting up an efficient home office will enable both of you to make the most of your time. And nowadays, with more companies downsizing and turning employees into independent contractors, having a workspace at home makes more sense than ever.

If the two of you think there isn't enough room in your home to devote exclusively to an office, consider the following options:

1. If you have a spare room that's been designated the "guest room," ask yourselves whether that's really the best use of the room. You may be better off setting up the space for an office that you'll probably use a lot more often than you'll have guests. (You can always keep a sofabed in there, too.)

2. All you really need in terms of space for a bare-bones, "low-tech" office setup is a work surface (it doesn't have to be a desk) and something in which to store files (it needn't be a file cabinet). There are cleverly designed hideaway office units (page 183) that open up to provide a desktop, file drawers and cubbyholes for supplies and which can be closed up when not in use.

3. You can create a portable home office setup with inexpensive products such as Fellowes' Neat Ideas Payment Center (page 183) and Rubbermaid's Box Office (page 183). Both units have handles for easy carrying, and you can stack them underneath a kitchen counter, for example, when not in use. They can be used in conjunction with the kitchen or dining-room table (which in many homes is the most popular place to do paperwork anyway).

The more equipment you use, the more space you'll need for your home office. Many high-tech products that used to be expensive have become so affordable that more and more couples are using them at home: Such items as computers, laser printers, modems, fax machines, photocopiers, paper shredders and cellular phones are becoming fairly commonplace in a variety of households. There's even a neat product on the market for novice com-

puter users who need to keep instructions and guidelines on how
to use the programs close at hand. It's called Corkboard Screenies
and it's a corkboard frame that fits around your monitor screen so
that you can tack notes and messages all around the perimeter.
(See page 183.)

The checklists on this and the following page provide guidelines for setting up a more high-tech workspace.

---

10 CRUCIAL AREAS

— Desk or work surface
— Computer hutch/surface
— Printer stand/surface
— File storage: drawer, cabinet, cart, portable filebox,
   desktop file holder, over-the-door storage, wall holder,
   archive storage box
— Supplies storage: desktop, drawers, shelves, cabinets
— Paper-sorting surface
— Telephone and answering machine area
— Fax area
— Photocopier station
— Reference/resources   section: bookshelves,   journal
   holders

12 ARRANGEMENT/ENVIRONMENT CONSIDERATIONS

— Lighting
— Noise level
— Temperature
— Location of primary work surface
— Size of work surface
— Height of work surface
— Comfort of chair
— Location of wastebasket

___ Accessibility of active files
___ Accessibility of frequently used supplies
___ Clock within easy viewing distance
___ Calendar within easy view/reach

FURNISHINGS/ACCESSORIES   EQUIPMENT

___ Bookcase/shelves   ___ Phone answering system
___ Chair   ___ Cellular phone
___ Computer hutch   ___ Computer
___ Desk/work surface unit(s)   ___ Copy machine
___ Lamp   ___ Fax machine
___ Magnetic board or wipe-off   ___ Modem
    board
___ Paper cutter   ___ Paper shredder
___ Printer stand   ___ Printer
___ File storage unit   ___ Telephone
___ Wastebasket   ___ Typewriter

OFFICE SUPPLIES

Interestingly, it seems that both men and women like to buy office supplies—sometimes in staggering quantities. (I call this the "Discount Warehouse Syndrome.")

Overloading on office supplies is easy to do since many of the products seem inexpensive, but they add up quickly—and they can take up a lot of space. If you and your mate stockpile little boxes of paperclips, pads of Post-its, bottles of correction fluid, reams of paper, legal pads, and mugs filled with pens, there won't be room to get any office work done—let alone enough space to fulfill your fantasies of making love on a desktop.

Office supply overstock can be avoided by sticking to these three steps:

1. Have only two places for supplies: An area on or in your desk or work-space should be allocated for frequently used supplies, and a cabinet, credenza or other storage area can be designated for backups and refills.

2. Use a master list for purchasing supplies that are running low (see next page). Post it next to the supplies storage area so that it can be used like a shopping list—remember, put a checkmark next to items on the list that are running low.

3. Don't purchase office products on impulse; bring your master list with you and buy only in reasonable quantities.

   If your home office is already clogged with the types of items described above, and you don't have sufficient storage space for the excess, consider donating the overstock to a nonprofit organization. You can write it off on your taxes. Then at least it will do someone else some good—unless, of course, you and your mate have waited too long and the paperclips have rusted, the white-out is caked solid and the pens have dried up (all of which happen when you overbuy these supplies).

   Sherry's husband Bill had the annoying habit of borrowing her office supplies and not returning them. Occasionally, he would lose them. After several arguments about this they came up with a solution. They hung a "Borrowing Board" (wipe-off board or cork-board) on the office wall and established the rule that neither of them could borrow something without first making a note of it on the board. The borrower also must agree to return the borrowed item within 24 hours or he or she will have to provide a duplicate of the item. Because the borrowed item is posted on the board, the borrowed-from mate can at least follow up on the borrower before an item disappears for an extended time. This solution may sound a little drastic, but it worked for Bill and Sherry.

BASIC HOME OFFICE SUPPLIES

ONE-TIME PURCHASES	ONGOING PURCHASES
Address file	Computer disks
Calculator	Computer disk organizer(s)
Clock	Envelopes—manila, (large)
Paper clip dispenser	and #10
Pencil sharpener	Fax paper
Postal scale	File supplies*
Scissors	Highlighters
Stapler	Legal pads
Staple remover	Paper clips
Surge protector	Pens & pencils
Tape dispenser	Staples
Three-hole punch	

*Hanging files, interior files, file tabs, file labels

ADDRESSES, PHONE NUMBERS, BUSINESS CARDS...

Togetherness as a couple does not always extend to your address books. It's rare for even the most loving pair to have one shared system for keeping track of phone numbers, addresses and business cards. Generally speaking, each mate has his or her own list of frequently called numbers—friends, family, business contacts and services—so having separate systems is one logical option. Whichever system you use, however, should be able to pass the "simple, flexible, growth-oriented" test. For example, bound (non-loose-leaf) address books aren't flexible or growth oriented, so no matter how cute they look, shun them—you'll avoid the future hell of having to spend hours transferring information into a new system. There are far more pleasant ways to spend that time.

> "Money . . . was exactly like sex. You thought of nothing else if you didn't have it and thought of other things if you did."
>
> — JAMES BALDWIN

These days there are plenty of good systems from which to choose: card file systems (such as Rolodex), computer programs (such as Address Book Plus) and business card loose-leaf books and related systems all offer simple, flexible, growth-oriented options that couples can use to save time and minimize friction. (An excellent resource for information and products relating to this topic is *Organized to Be the Best!*; see Recommended Reading section, page 189.)

If you and your mate would prefer to share one system, a color-coded Rolodex is one surprisingly simple and effective yet low-tech option that works well for couples. Rolodex Transparent Card Protectors, made to slip over individual cards (see page 183), come in a rainbow of colors, but you'll probably only need to choose two—one color for you and one for your mate. Shared cards, such as those for repair services, doctors, etc., can be kept sleeveless. Grouping each mate's Rolodex cards together and using the protectors to color each section of the system make it easy to see at a glance whose cards are whose. You can also get the Rolodex cards themselves in several colors, but using the removable protectors provides for greater flexibility if you decide to change things. The protectors also help to keep the cards from becoming frayed. If you choose a Rolodex that accommodates 3-inch-by-5-inch cards, you can affix business cards to the Rolodex cards without having to trim or mutilate them to make them fit—another timesaver.

BILLS

Paying bills may be at the top of the list of thankless chores. It's one of the most hated jobs that many couples face, and probably causes more fights than any other chore. Who does what when and what procedures does he or she use? Do you pay each bill as it arrives, or wait and pay them all together once or twice a month? When there are two incomes, who pays for what?

Whether you pay the bills together, or one of you does it alone, there's bound to be some frustration involved. Setting up a simple, easy-to-use system for bill paying will help take some of the pain out of the task.

But first, you must decide who will pay the bills. Maybe one of you actually wants to take over the whole job. Great. If not, you have the option of setting aside some time each month to work together on it, taking turns, or maybe hiring a bookkeeper. One couple I worked with found that when they tried working together on this task they always ended up yelling at each other. So, they worked out a system where she pays the bills for six months, then he takes over and does it for the next six months. They find this method keeps things more peaceful around the house.

TIMING

The day of the month on which you choose to pay your bills can make a difference in how onerous a chore it is. Some people, usually those who have few bills to pay, find it easier to just pay the bills as they arrive. That way they run little risk of forgetting to pay any, thus avoiding unnecessary late charges. For others, that method doesn't work. The key is to establish a bill-paying routine and stick with it.

Vicki is the designated bill payer in her family—not because she's particularly adept at it. It just happened that she was between jobs when she and Jake married. So, since she had time on her hands, she took on the family finances. Fourteen years later she's still stuck with the task, and he claims financial ignorance. But it works.

Each month, she writes between 50 and 60 checks. Probably half of these are written to pay bills, which arrive in the mailbox at an almost daily rate. Each one, depending on where it originates, has a different due date, which means it's not feasible to pay all the bills only once a month. In the case of Vicki and Jake, he

> *"I find it more trouble to take care of money than to get it."*
> — MONTAIGNE

is on salary and gets paid every two weeks. She, on the other hand, is an independent contractor and gets paid as she completes each project. So for them, paying the bills at least twice a month makes sense. To do this, Vicki created a file marked "Bills to Be Paid." In this file are four manila folders marked: "Week 2," "Week 4," "Rental," and "Business." The last two folders are separate because those bills are paid out of separate checking accounts, and are paid only once a month. As bills arrive, she puts them in the appropriate folder. Then, twice a month, she sits down, opens the folder, and pays each bill.

If you dislike the taste of glue, a product such as the Secretariat (see page 183) can really add efficiency to this part of bill paying. This neat little unit will affix stamps, seal envelopes, and even open letters, with little effort on your part. You can also purchase just the postage stamp affixer. Another time-saver is to use preprinted return address labels or a pre-inked stamper. I'm amazed by people who laboriously write their return address on each envelope. Frankly, I have better things to do— don't you?

HIGH TECH OPTIONS

If you own a home computer and you haven't yet purchased personal finance software, you might consider it. Programs such as Intuit's Quicken can make financial chores much easier. These programs are usually easy to use and are probably one of the biggest time savers you can buy. With them you can: pay bills, track investments, keep tax records automatically, track credit card spending, create budgets and print out a variety of reports. They also memorize transactions so that you don't have to type in the same names on the checks each month. In fact, they can memorize whole groups of transactions, and then with a few keystrokes instruct the computer to pay those bills. And if you are the forgetful type, many programs will display an icon when you turn on your computer to remind you that it's time to pay certain bills.

> *"Money would be more enjoyable if it took people as long to spend it as it does to earn it."*
> — ED HOWE

Quicken, and programs like it, also offer check printing capabilities. Rather than having to handwrite your checks each month you just tell the computer which bills you want to pay, and the amount. Once you've verified the checks are correct, you can instruct the printer to print on special preprinted checks, which have an area for return addresses. Then you sign your checks, stick them in a special double-window envelope and off they go.

If even that is too much trouble, you can use an electronic check-writing feature. This lets you fill out your various checks on the computer; then after calling a special phone number with your computer's modem, the software can automatically send your checks where they need to go via the phone line. No envelopes, no stamps, no hassle.

CHECKING ACCOUNT OPTIONS

Deciding which types of checking and savings accounts you and your mate will have is an important issue. Some couples, like Henry and me, find it works best to each have a separate account. We also have a joint account, but it rarely gets used. Vicki and Jake, on the other hand, have several joint accounts (four checking, three savings), each designated for certain uses. How you and your mate decide to establish your accounts will really depend on your individual lifestyle and financial needs.

Many personal finance programs link up to tax preparation software so you can also prepare your own taxes relatively painlessly. And with the time and money you save by using these programs, you and your sweetie can go on a romantic getaway.

Once you've used one of these programs, you'll wonder how you ever lived without it. Imagine trying to go back to a typewriter after using a word processor.

BUDGETS

Even if you and your mate are independently wealthy, you're probably going to have to live by some type of budget or spending plan. Some personalities love budgeting. They get a thrill from planning out exactly what their income is and where each penny goes. Then there are the rest of us. Whether you like it or not, a good spending plan will free you from the slavery of unplanned and unorganized spending habits.

Jerry and Paula, a teacher and a librarian, live a somewhat loosely budgeted life. Thanks to the personal finance software they use, they have a detailed record of exactly where their money goes. Using this program, they have determined just how much money they need to survive each month, including a regular deposit to their retirement account. They have also established their own impound account, a separate savings account where they accumulate funds to pay for mortgage payments, insurance premiums, vehicle registrations, property taxes and other expenses that must be paid on a regular basis. Just knowing the money will be there when the bill is due has made them feel more relaxed about their financial situation.

You don't need a computer, however, to keep track of your finances. If you and your partner will spend an hour or two putting together a spending plan and then update it once a month, you may find you'll spend less time worrying about money and paying the bills, leaving more time to enjoy other types of figures.

Start by listing all the sources of income you both have. Then make a list of every single expense you might encounter during the year. The list on page 44 should get you started.

Once you've determined exactly what your income and expenses are, plan your spending strategy for each month. Be sure to include in your expenses any money you put toward savings or retirement.

INCOMING MAIL

It's important for couples to discuss appropriate ways to process incoming mail so that privacy is respected and important pieces aren't lost or accidentally tossed. Agree on a central location where the mail can be safely deposited each day by whoever brings it in. If the mail is just left in a haphazard heap in a different spot each day, things are apt to get confusing. Set up a basket or tray to be used expressly for incoming mail (you may want to label it, too) and put it in a logical spot.

For example, if a corner of the kitchen counter seems to be where the mail gets dumped, locate the "mail processing center" there. A letter opener placed next to the basket will facilitate opening envelopes; try the Presto (page 184), or you may prefer to use an electronic letter opener (available at most stationery stores) to make the process more efficient as well as more enjoyable.

Hot Tip: Some of these little gadgets are actually fun to use and therefore help to increase your "5% joy" quotient by making the maintenance aspect of life more pleasurable.

Before we were married, Henry had a tendency to let mail pile up unopened and he rarely got around to tossing even the most obviously junky junk mail. But after we rehabilitated his house I suggested a different way to handle the mail. To insure that

> *"The United States has the greatest variety of postage stamps, but they all taste the same."*
> — ANONYMOUS

SPENDING PLAN LIST

INCOME SOURCES	EXPENSES
Wages or Salary	Auto: Gas/Oil
Bonuses	Auto: Loan
Commissions	Auto: Repairs/Maintenance
Fees	Bank Charges
Rents	Beauty/Barber
Dividends and Interest	Cable TV
Royalties	Classes
Tips	Clothes
Child Support	Contribution or Tithe
Alimony	Credit Card Payments
Other _____	Gifts/Birthdays/Etc.
	Goals (One Year—i.e., new car, down payment for house)
	Groceries
	Household Supplies
	Income Taxes
	Insurance: Auto
	Insurance: Health
	Insurance: Home
	Insurance: Life
	Laundry/Dry Cleaning
	Meals Out (lunches/dinners)
	Medical: Doctor/Dentist/Etc.
	Memberships: (Clubs/Organizations)
	Mortgage Payment/Rent
	Music
	Personal Loans
	Property Taxes
	Reserve Savings
	Retirement Plan (IRA or Other)
	Social Security Deductions (if you work for yourself)
	Sports
	Student Loans
	Sundries
	Subscriptions: Mags/Newspapers
	Telephone: Local & Long Distance
	Theaters
	Vacations
	Utilities: Gas/Electric/Water/Sewer

this happened, I set up a mail-processing area right next to the mail slot by the front door. The area consists of a small table which has just enough surface area to hold a basket and a Presto letter opener. Tucked conveniently yet unobtrusively below the table is a wastebasket. This type of arrangement makes it easier for Henry to process the mail. (Of course, where the mail goes after it's been opened is also important; see Chapter Four for suggestions on setting up paper-flow and action-file systems.)

THE QUICKEST WAY TO PROCESS MAIL

1. Stand next to wastebasket or recycling system. (Note: It's been demonstrated that decisions are made more quickly while standing.)

2. Using a letter opener, slit open each envelope.

3. Immediately discard all obvious junk mail, as well as extraneous items such as advertising inserts and outer envelopes.

4. Categorize what's left, either by mate (one stack for each of you) or by grouping together such items as bills, correspondence, magazines/newsletters, catalogs, etc., in separate stacks or in a paper-flow or action-file system (see Chapter Four).

5. Try to get rid of catalogs as quickly as possible—if you can't leaf through them quickly while standing there, put them in a basket or upright holder next to a favorite seat (this can be the commode) and be sure to have a "mini-office" basket with highlighter, pens, Post-it flags, calculator, etc., placed nearby.

If you receive a neighbor's mail by accident, be courteous and take it to them immediately (even if they're not your favorite people). Or leave it out for your mail carrier to redeliver. This may seem obvious, but it's surprising how often people don't get around to passing along misdelivered mail.

As in other areas of couplehood, respecting each other's privacy is something that should be taken into account when opening mail. Early on in our marriage, Henry and I agreed on the following arrangement:

1. Whoever comes home first gets to open the mail.
2. If what looks like a personal letter or card is addressed to one name only, it will be opened only by the one whose name is on the envelope.
3. The only mail to be discarded without consulting the other person is stuff that is addressed to "Resident" or junk mail addressed to the people who lived at the house five years ago.

However you and your spouse agree to handle incoming mail, be clear about what constitutes an invasion of privacy to each of you. If one of you has concerns about what may seem like overly secretive behavior, especially regarding financial matters or mysterious valentines, it should be discussed and resolved; sometimes a third party such as a marriage counselor can help.

TELEPHONE MESSAGES

If a mate is absent-minded about taking messages, he or she can unwittingly create chaos and angry episodes. Forgetting to tell your spouse that someone called for them is generally inexcusable (with the possible exception of a call from an old flame). Sometimes the problem lies in not having a convenient message system in place by each phone. A pen and a pad of paper may be adequate as long as there's a way of getting them to stay where they belong because there's a tendency for them to migrate. Unless there's a systematic way of noting and posting messages, what often happens is that a note is scribbled without a date and then is left to be found by accident—hours or days later. Depending on the relative importance of the aging message, complaints and accusations can fly—not exactly conducive to romantic readiness.

One logical step is to set up a convenient and effective "message center." This can be done by putting up a bulletin board, a wipe-off board, or a combination of the two, in a hard-to-miss location such as on the back of the entry door or on the front of the refrigerator. The Post-it Memo-board (page 184), a thin sheet of plasticized material covered with re-stickable adhesive, also functions as a bulletin board, only no tacks or pushpins are needed: Notes adhere automatically to the surface yet they are still easily removable.

> *"The prenatal period is the only time in a person's life when his name cannot be found on a mailing list."*
>
> — ANONYMOUS

Designate one part of the message center for telephone message notes—for example, the upper right-hand corner—and the rest of the space can be used for reminders, shopping lists and love notes (not necessarily in that order). Be sure to keep a notepad and pen or pencil nearby—you may want to attach them to the message center with stout chains, if you or your mate have demonstrated a tendency to walk off with them. And remember to toss or erase old messages regularly, otherwise your message center will begin to resemble the Great Wall of Clutter.

If you've ever misplaced a phone message note—your own or someone else's—you know it can cause frustration and friction. To avoid this, consider using a spiral-bound telephone message book with carbonless copies; tie a pen onto the spiral with a string, and you have a practically foolproof way of capturing messages. Tying the message book to the surface where you want it to stay can ensure that it won't roam. This can be done by attaching another string from the spiral to a table leg or similar furnishing. I got one for Henry and we were both delighted with the results: He writes down messages on the forms, tears them out and promptly loses them—but thanks to the carbonless system, he no longer wastes time looking for the crumpled scraps. He can even refer back to messages that came in months ago, since the book functions as a record-keeping system for him as well. And the forms make it easy for him to remember to take down the date and time of a call as well as the name and phone number of the caller.

If you've tried these various solutions and your mate is still neglecting to pass on phone messages, consider installing separate phone lines. Then agree not to answer each other's phones except in the case of an emergency. Separate answering machines or voice mail can also help to eliminate potential problems. I worked with one couple who actually invested in three lines: his, hers and theirs. Although these options may cost more in dollars, they can save time and cut down on the stress caused by misplaced and garbled messages.

TAXES AND RECORD KEEPING

When it comes to doing your taxes, the best way to save time is to keep good records—and don't wait until the end of March to collect those records. Keep them up to date throughout the year. For those couples who have trouble doing this, I recommend a very basic, simplistic approach: At the beginning of the new year, get a large file box and mark it "Taxes (Year)." Then as you and your mate collect receipts for deductible items or other tax-related papers, put them in the file box. The following January, when you begin receiving W-2 forms and 1099's, paper clip them together and add them to the file box. If you save paid invoices and bank statements, you can also add these to the box every few months. When tax season arrives, you'll already have everything in one place, which will make the process easier.

If you use a personal finance computer program, much of your tax work will probably be done for you. These programs can record transactions by various categories, so that at the year's end you can print a report telling just how much you earned and how much was spent on tax deductible items. If you hire an accountant to do your taxes, these reports can go straight to him or her.

> *"Money isn't everything; in fact after the tax collector gets through, money isn't anything."*
> — ANONYMOUS

HEALTH INSURANCE

If you're lucky enough to work for an employer who offers medical/dental benefits, you may have the sometimes frustrating experience of dealing with claim forms. Currently, the variety of employer-sponsored insurance programs is astounding, and each program has its own way of doing business. In many instances, however, there will be some type of form to fill out in order to get your money reimbursed. Getting a system in place to track these claim forms will not only save you time, but maybe even some money. By carefully checking a hospital bill, Vicki once found a $350 error.

If you follow the advice in Chapter Four on setting up a filing system, you'll have a place to put your insurance paperwork. To make filing claims easy, you may want to create a separate file for each of you. I also suggest a file marked "Claims Sent." Once you've copied a medical bill and sent the duplicate to your insurer, place a Post-it note marked with the date on the original and put it in this file. Mark your calendar to remind you to follow up periodically to insure that claims are being paid promptly. When a claim is paid, record the amount received on a list of medical/dental expenses and reimbursements, and drop the Explanation of Benefits form into the appropriate person's insurance file. At the end of the year, you'll have a record of how much was spent and how much was reimbursed.

Another tip for saving time is to pre-address some envelopes with the insurance company's name. That way when you're hurrying to file a claim, you won't have to search for an envelope and the address. It also may be helpful to keep some partially completed claim forms on hand. Fill in the employee's name, address and other general information. Then leave the patient section to be filled in when you use it.

HOUSEHOLD INVENTORY

Making an extensive list of all the items you own doesn't sound like a timesaving project. But, should you ever have a fire or other type of loss, you'll be grateful you took the time to make that list.

You can do a simple pen-and-paper inventory by walking through the house and noting all the furniture, appliances, stereo equipment, jewelry and other items of value you own. Or, if you own a video camera, you can go around the house with your mate and videotape these same items, verbally telling what each item is worth as you tape it. Not too adept with a camera? In many cities you can hire a video company to provide this service for you. Just be sure to check references—you don't want to provide the local hoodlums with a guided tour of your home.

4

Putting Paper in Its Place

"*D*on't touch that pile!"

Anyone who has ever lived with someone who has a chronic case of "paperosis displacea" has heard this pitiful cry. And woe to any mate who doesn't heed it! Straightening, neatening, rearranging, moving or tossing the contents of someone else's piles of paper is tantamount to vandalism—it produces only feelings of violation, victimization and, ultimately, anger and seething resentment.

When you're sharing any type of space with your "significant other," paper problems can loom large. Consider some of the typical categories of paper that the two of you may be confronting on a regular basis: Bills (paid and unpaid), bank statements (and cancelled checks), brochures and fliers, business cards, cartoons, catalogs, coupons, correspondence, instructions and warranties, legal documents, lists, magazines, newspapers, notes, receipts, recipes, tax records . . . the list goes on.

It's hard enough to stay on top of your own papers, let alone someone else's. So it's not surprising that paper clutter is often a major source of arguments and stress for couples. (Sometimes both mates generate piles, but only one of them is actually bothered by the perceived problem and therefore tends to blame the other for it.)

If your mate is the prime source of paper piles in your household, it can be helpful to understand why it's so difficult for them to deal with their piles.

DECISION-MAKING VERSUS LETTING GO

In general, paper pile-o-maniacs tend to have one or both of the following traits:

1. A perceived inability to make decisions
2. Difficulty letting things go

Of the two, the first is usually easier to conquer than the second. For example, Henry has trouble making decisions but doesn't really agonize over throwing or giving things away. So I discovered a way to keep his paper piles to a minimum (at least outside The Pit).

First of all, I never discard any of his papers without getting his permission. Whenever I find some paper he's left on the dining-room table, kitchen counter, etc., that looks "tossable," I wait till he's available (usually before dinner) and then hold the item in front of him and ask, "Can we discard this?" Usually he answers yes. When he answers no, I ask, "Where would you like to keep it?" Depending on his response, I do one of three things: file it in my household filing system, put it in Henry's filing system, or toss it on the floor of The Pit and shut the door (sometimes resisting the urge to slam it).

By asking Henry specific, nonjudgmental questions on just one piece of paper at a time, I help him to focus and therefore make a decision. If you overwhelm your mate with more than one thing at a time, he or she may become sidetracked and frustrated, and the decision-making process will most likely become even more agonizing. Likewise, if you use a sarcastic or impatient tone, your beloved may very well tune you out or become angry and hostile.

If your mate has difficulty letting things go—he or she is afraid that "once I throw it out, I'll need it/miss it/find out it was valuable," etc.—it can be helpful to deal with his or her papers on a more pragmatic level, by asking questions such as: "If you want to keep every issue of *Consumer Reports,* and you receive 12 issues a year, and 12 issues equals three inches of shelf space, how many shelves can we afford to allocate to *Consumer Reports?*" Or, "If we transfer your old college term papers to a file box in the garage, we won't need to buy another file cabinet. What do you think?"

By approaching the problem logically, the issue of letting go can become less of a focus. If you can help your mate shift his attention from the fear of letting go to some realistic options for dealing with his papers, you may start to see some positive changes. Likewise, if you can demonstrate in dollars how much money could be saved by more efficient paper-handling techniques, it's possible that he'll be more enthusiastic about the process. Although time *isn't* money (as I stated in Chapter One), some people have difficulty placing a value on it unless it is defined in monetary terms.

The following worksheet demonstrates how much money is wasted by disorganized paperwork.

SEE HOW MUCH MONEY YOU'RE LOSING BY
WASTING TIME ON PAPERWORK

Your wage per hour $ ____
(Note: If you are salaried or do not otherwise earn a set dollar amount per hour, estimate what you feel your time is worth.)

How much time do you spend per day:
- Locating papers? _____ (minutes/hours)
- Looking for misplaced items? _____
- Being aggravated because you can't find things? _____
- Duplicating efforts? _____
- Procrastinating? _____

Total wasted time per day ____ × $ ____ Hourly wage = $ ____ × 5 days per week = $ ____ × 4 weeks per month = $ ____ × 12 months = $ ____ wasted per year

THE FIVE TYPES OF PILES

Piles of paper, if left alone, will breed at an alarming rate.

According to my research, there are actually five types of piles:

1. *The Growing Pile:* It keeps getting higher and higher (especially if the mail isn't processed daily or if someone in your household subscribes to numerous publications). Everything from unopened mail to bills to receipts to newspaper clippings to business cards to brochures to insurance papers to take-out menus will feed its growth.
2. *The Stagnating Pile:* This used to be a Growing Pile until its growth was abruptly stunted, generally when it was hastily shoved into a bag, box, drawer, closet, cabinet or under the bed—usually because someone was coming over.
3. *The Diminishing Pile:* This is the pile that shows progress—it's getting smaller because someone is actually dealing with it instead of adding to it or hiding it away.
4. *The Distilled Pile:* This pile has gone through the previous three stages only to grind to a halt when its contents have been sifted down to sediment—the last few hard pieces of paper that seem impervious to the decision-making process. These are the papers that get shuffled and reshuffled endlessly because you feel as though you "can't decide" what to do with them (and you're never ready to just toss them out).
5. *The Double-Distilled Pile*: This occurs when there are several little Distilled Piles lying around and—in some pathetic, misguided effort to "clean up"—you sweep them all together and create one monstrous pile that seems completely impenetrable because you've already reshuffled the contents thousands of times and are no closer to making a decision than you were the first time.

THE INFORMATION AGE

Now that we are firmly entrenched in the Information Age, paper has become the modern Medusa, multiplying on desktops and dining-room tables alike at a horrifying rate. Consider the following factoids:

- The amount of paper generated by U.S. businesses doubles every four years.
- The average person spends eight months in the course of a lifetime just opening junk mail.
- Most people waste 30 minutes every day just looking for papers that are lost on their desktops.

Yet paper management skills aren't taught in primary or secondary schools, and it's rare to find any college courses on the topic (although private adult schools such as The Learning Annex offer them).

THREE SYSTEMS

There are three systems that, used together, will help you and your mate keep papers under control. They are the time management system, the paper-flow or action-file system, and the filing system.

The time management system is discussed in Chapter One. It's crucial for each half of a couple to have an effective one. It's equally important for the two of you to schedule a regular weekly "planning ritual" together. Sundays (a.m. or p.m.) can be ideal for this, but any day is good that consistently works well for both of you. Sit down with your calendars, planners, appointment books or whatever systems you're currently using for time management, and discuss what each of you plan to accomplish over the next week. Be sure to schedule at least one "date night" with each other.

Early on in a close relationship, one person usually takes over the bulk of the paperwork management—either voluntarily or by default. When this is the case, it is often effective for that mate to schedule a block of time each week for paper maintenance. The paper-related systems that will need to be maintained are the paper-flow or action-file system and the filing system.

SETTING UP A PAPER-FLOW OR ACTION-FILE SYSTEM

"Action papers," such as bills to pay, correspondence to answer, and forms to complete, need an accessible holding place that keeps the different categories of "to do's" separate so you don't have to paw through piles looking for things. When you sit down to do your paper maintenance, you want to be able to instantly locate the papers you planned to read, fill out or file.

Depending on your aesthetics and personal styles, there are different options for creating systems to hold action papers. A *paper-flow system* is usually set up with stacking trays or baskets—one for each category of paper, and each labeled clearly with the name of the category (such as Bills, Correspondence, To Read, etc.). An *action-file system* can be set up in a file holder (a plastic device made to hold only about a dozen or so files and designed to sit on a desktop or table or fit inside a file drawer; see page 184), with each file clearly labeled with the name of the category (like the ones used for the paper-flow system).

It really doesn't matter which variation of the system you use. My criteria for any good system are that it must be simple, flexible and growth oriented. Whatever you can use comfortably and consistently is a good system. Also, both members of a couple need to be able to find papers easily—not just the one who deals with them most of the time. In case of an emergency (or a semi-emergency), it should be easy to explain to someone over the phone where to locate the property tax bill that needs to be mailed today, for example.

Bear in mind that whatever type of system you choose needs to have a limited number of

> *"We are involved in a life that passes understanding and our highest business is our daily life."*
>
> — *JOHN CAGE*

broad categories (probably no more than eight to 10), clearly labeled. Check out the following list of action-paper categories for ideas:

Bills to Pay
Catalogs/Ads
Correspondence
Coupons
Events/Invitations
Pending
To Do (General)
To File
To Read
Show to _____ (mate's name)

Stacking trays can be found at office supply stores as well as office supply departments of various drugstores and department stores. The advantages to using these trays include:

High visibility. Since stacking trays take up more space than files, they are harder to ignore and it's more likely that someone will put things in the trays instead of heaping them in a pile somewhere. Of course, effective placement is important. Depending on the available areas in your home (and your style) your paper-flow system could be located anywhere, from a desktop in your home office to the corner of the kitchen counter where the mail usually collects (often an ideal spot).

Stacking trays work best for people who are highly visual—those who always like to *see* where things are. (That's why they often have piles of paper—they don't want to put anything away for fear they'll never find it again!)

Ease of access. Stacking trays are user-friendly, especially for those who are unaccustomed to using files. It's easier to throw something in a labeled stacking tray than to locate the correct folder.

Efficient use of vertical space. Since stacking trays are

stackable, eight will take up the same amount of desk or counter space as just one.

Action-file systems work best for people who have:

1. Very limited space.
2. Experience using files.
3. An aversion to "having stuff out."

Action files can be set up in a variety of portable file holders (see page 57). If you have plenty of file drawers, you can forgo the file holder and just locate your action files in the front of the most easily accessible file drawer. It's a good idea to use colored files—red, for example—for these action files so as to clearly separate them from any other files in the drawer.

Labeling the files or stack trays in a clear, easy-to-read manner is crucial. If neither of you can read each other's scrawl, you may want to splurge on one of the nifty new labeling machines currently on the market (see page 184). For under a hundred dollars you can get what looks and functions like a mini-computer/printer, which prints out beautiful adhesive-backed labels in a variety of styles, sizes and colors. These labelers come in handy for everything from organizing your files to labeling shelves in the linen closet to indicate where different items should be put away. (Especially handy when you're training a mate to put things away where they belong . . . see Chapter Five.) Of course, if you have a computer and laser printer you can create labels too, but you may have to cut them to size, unless you get a labeler attachment (see page 184).

USING THE SYSTEM

Now that you've set up your labeled stacking trays or action files, you need to be aware of the following fact: The system will not *do* the papers for you! This means if you keep stuffing papers in the stacking trays or files without ever actually removing any, you'll wind up with packaged "piles." Unless you get in the habit of setting aside time on a weekly basis to take action on the papers that you and your mate put in the system, the system will not work. Systems that are not maintained invariably fail.

If both of you have trouble handling paperwork, you may want to try setting up a weekly (or biweekly) paper processing ritual together. Whether you face each other across the dining room table or sit companionably side-by-side in matching La-Z-Boy recliners as you read, write and mumble, knowing that your mate is shouldering her or his share of the burden can make the process less unpleasant. It's often effective to set a time limit (usually anywhere from 30 minutes to an hour is sufficient) and plan a reward (use your Rewards Ideas List from Chapter One).

Okay, you're processing the papers from your action-paper system—paying bills, clipping coupons, answering correspondence, reading newsletters. As you complete each task, you'll be left with a piece of paper and usually a choice between two options: toss it or file it. (I'm talking about what's left after you've prepared the bills, letters, etc., to mail.)

The more stuff you decide to toss, the less you'll have to file. There are basically just two types of paper to file: records and resources. Records are the papers we *have* to keep (for purposes such as identification or the IRS); resources are the papers we *want* to keep. There is a crucial difference between these two types of paper when it comes to space: Records tend to be finite in quantity in that there is only a limited number of records to file over the course of a year; resources, on the other hand, can be infinite in quantity. They are limited only by your imagination and how quickly you can clip things out of newspapers, magazines and catalogs or accumulate such items as brochures, fliers and maps.

Let's look at five realistic examples of some common kinds of paper you and your mate might be confronting on a regular basis, with suggestions on how to handle them.

PAID BILLS

You don't need to keep all of your paid bill stubs. Bill stubs for things like cable TV, bottled water delivery and newspaper subscriptions can be tossed after paying them (although you may want to keep the most current one until the next month's arrives, just to make sure you've been credited properly). Credit card statements, insurance payments, utility bills and mortgage payments may be kept on file for one year; at the end of the year, whatever isn't needed for tax or legal purposes can be tossed, and the remainder transferred into archival storage (cardboard file boxes work well for this; see Chapter Three for more storage options).

BANK STATEMENTS AND CANCELED CHECKS

It's not uncommon these days for couples to have at least three checking accounts between them. That can add up to a lot of checks, not to mention 36 statements per year. The simplest way to deal with these statements (although not necessarily the most efficient) is to keep each one folded around the batch of checks that came with it (it's even okay to keep them in the envelope) and file it in chronological order, grouping each account's statements together. It's perfectly all right to use shoe boxes or similar containers, or you can file them in hanging box-files (see page 184). At the end of each year they can be transferred into archival storage (check with your tax preparer or the IRS for current rules).

CORRESPONDENCE

Except for correspondence relating to legal and financial matters, most letters and cards can be discarded unless you or your mate are sentimental. If at least one of you is reluctant to toss anything from old love letters to ancient birthday cards, you may want to get a trunk or "memory chest" for storing such mementos. (Don't make fun of someone else's sentimentality, by the way. It probably won't convince them to throw out anything, and might just cause them

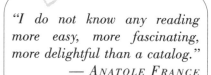

"I do not know any reading more easy, more fascinating, more delightful than a catalog."
— *ANATOLE FRANCE*

hurt feelings and resentment. Of course, if they're saving love letters from an old flame, disregard this advice.) Regular weeding is essential, unless you want to keep investing in storage containers for memorabilia.

CATALOGS AND MAGAZINES

Depending on how many mailing lists the two of you are on and how many subscriptions you have, catalogs and magazines can create molehills or mountains of clutter. Decide how much of this glossy garbage each of you is allowed to keep at any given time, and allocate space accordingly. It makes sense to keep all bound materials stored vertically instead of piled horizontally; plastic or cardboard upright journal holders will each hold at least a dozen issues of a publication and can be kept on a shelf or counter. Of course, if you and/or your mate suffer from what I call "subscribitus," you will never have enough space to keep all your publications—unless you keep moving to larger and larger homes. (In fact, one of my clients purchased the house next door to where they lived just to store their clutter overflow.)

COUPONS

These days there are coupons for everything: grocery items, restaurants, carwash, shoe repair, film developing, carpet cleaning—every kind of product or service seems to have gotten in on the act. If you and your mate actually do use coupons regularly or occasionally, good for you. However, if you just keep stockpiling them but never seem to get around to using them, then you probably are getting along just fine without them (although they may be creating clutter for you). If your mate thinks coupons are a nuisance, or doesn't give a hoot whether you use them or not—and if you rarely remember to use them yourself—get in the habit of tossing them as soon as they arrive. Should you actually use coupons (or seriously plan to), the Jokari Coupon Organizer (page 184) is a well-designed, easy-to-carry system for keeping them organized.

SEVEN STEPS FOR SUCCESSFUL COUPONING

1. Establish a positive attitude: Think of couponing as a profitable hobby.

2. Set aside sufficient time on at least a weekly basis to clip and sort coupons in a leisurely fashion.

3. To make your couponing ritual pleasant and efficient, make sure you have the following:
   a. A comfortable chair
   b. Adequate lighting
   c. An uncluttered, spacious surface on which to put the coupons. (Laps don't count!)

4. Sort coupons into your coupon organizer either immediately as you clip them, or at the end of each "coupon session." (If yours is the latter style, then at least sort coupons into "Food" and "Non-Food" stacks as you go along; this will save you time later.) Avoid leaving a pile of "coupons to be sorted later"— procrastination = clutter!

5. If you clip a coupon you'd like to use on your next shopping trip, the following two steps are recommended:
   a. Write a "C" next to each item on your shopping list for which you have a coupon.
   b. Slip the coupon into the "Today's Purchases" slot in your coupon organizer.

6. ALWAYS bring your coupon organizer with you when you shop.

7. Periodically (monthly) weed through your coupon organizer to discard expired coupons and note coupons with upcoming expiration dates. Move these to your "Today's Purchases" section and note on your shopping list.

Do not become obsessive about using ALL coupons before they expire. If you occasionally miss a coupon deadline,
so what? There will always be more coupons!

Remember, couponing should be a fun and profitable
process—not a stressful, guilt-inducing, clutter-producing
chore. If you're not enjoying it and profiting from it, don't do
it.

THE DREADED "TO DO'S"

The secret to keeping the **Pending, Events/Invitations and To
Do** stack trays and files from becoming hideous black holes of paper can be summed up in two words: Follow up. Any time a piece
of paper is deposited in one of these categories, a follow-up or
deadline note should be penciled into your time management system or calendar. Example: When something is ordered from a catalog and you are told it will arrive within 10 days, mark your
calendar. If you receive it on time, you can toss the paperwork; if
it doesn't arrive, retrieve the paperwork from Pending and follow
up.

By now, most people have discovered that the goal of handling each piece of paper only once is completely unrealistic. I
have found, however, that making a decision about a piece of paper only once is much more effective, especially if you write that
decision on the document. The following exercise is designed to
get you in the habit of making decisions quickly. It will teach you
how to handle a piece of paper right away instead of starting a pile
with it. Then, even if you touch that paper again, all you need to
do is follow through with what you've marked in the upper right-
hand corner, instead of putting it back in a pile. Get your mate to
do this exercise with you. Once you've both mastered this process,
you won't need to use this exercise anymore.

THE FIVE W'S OF CLUTTER CONTROL

When confronting a potential piece of clutter, ask yourself:

1. WHAT is this?
2. WHY would I want to keep it?
3. WHEN would I ever need it?
4. WHERE would I look for it?
5. WHO else might have it?

After you have made the decision to keep a particular piece of paper, mark the decision in pencil in the upper right-hand corner. For example, if it is something to be filed, print "FILE" and then, below it, print the name or category of the file. If this file does not exist yet, print "SET UP FILE" instead of "FILE." Then, put the piece of paper in your paper-flow action-file system (see page 57).

SETTING UP YOUR HOUSEHOLD FILING SYSTEM

You may have done everything together from sky-diving to hot-tubbing, from romantic dinners to kinky sex, but there's one special experience the two of you probably haven't shared yet: setting up your filing system. This is a particularly intimate act of togetherness (well maybe that's stretching it a bit) that I hope will bring you happiness, or at least organization, for many years to come.

So set aside a nice quiet block of time with your beloved, wriggle into your sexiest file-clerk duds, turn on some romantic music, but don't dim the lights. You're going to need them to see what you're doing.

Whether the two of you are setting up a filing system together from scratch (or from scraps, as the case may be) or melding two existing systems into one, the same process applies: Work from a list—you're less likely to create redundant files or useless file names. Start out by making a list of file names. If you're blending two existing systems, make a list of all the file names from both systems. If you're starting with no files, the chart on page 67 might help you get started.

There are two main steps to creating your new filing system: Planning and Doing. During the planning stage, you and your mate will create an outline on paper, based on the list you compile. Depending on how many files you anticipate needing, you'll either be able to structure your list into a very simple alphabetized system (if you only have about 20 files or so) or an easy-to-use categorized system. When you have your outline in place, you'll proceed to actually setting up the new files and transferring or filing the contents of the old files (or the piles, if that's what you have).

Sit down with your mate, a pencil and a ruled legal pad. If you're reorganizing a system and/or blending two systems, one of you can read off the names of the existing files while the other writes them down. As you go along, discuss whether each file name is a good one or not—is it easily comprehensible to both of you or can it be improved? For example, if your car records file is labeled "Automobile" but you and your mate now co-own a motorcycle and an RV along with a jeep, would "Vehicles" be a better name? Or do you prefer "Cars"? Perhaps one of you has a dog and the other has a parrot (and there are papers relating to both of them): A file labeled "Pets" might be more efficient than having two separate folders labeled "Bird" and "Bowser."

If you do agree on some file name changes, write those down on your list, either next to or indented below the existing file name. This way, when you're referring to your list later as you create new file labels, you'll be able to locate the actual file to be relabeled.

It's important not to allow yourselves to get sidetracked dur-

FINANCIAL	HOUSEHOLD	PERSONAL	GENERAL
Banking -Acct 1 -Acct 2 -Acct 3	Cars/Vehicles	Correspondence	Emergency
Bills Paid (12 Months)	Decorating Ideas	Family	Humor (Smile File)
Budget	Gardening Tips	Gift Ideas (wish lists)	Beauty & Fitness
Credit Cards (contracts/ receipts)	Household Hints (Cleaning/ organizing)	Mate 1	Entertainment
Insurance -Auto -Health -Property	Improvements	Mate 2	Health Information
Investments	Instructions/ Warranties	Medical Records	Holidays
Mortgage	Inventory	Resumes/Career Info.	Inspirational Quotes
Receipts	Repair & Main- tenance Records (gardeners/ handymen/etc.)		Recipes
Taxes -recent returns -donations			Resources (misc.)
			Restaurants
			Travel

Note: The indented file names indicate interior folders that go inside the hanging files.

ing this part of the process. There's a tendency for people to start reading everything they come across in their files or piles instead of moving forward with their list. This is where it can be especially helpful to have two people working together on this project instead of just one. You can prod each other along when one or the other of you starts to linger over a particularly interesting item, such as a lingerie catalog.

Once you have your list in hand, look it over and decide whether a straight A-to-Z system will suffice or if it would be more helpful to group related files under broad categories such as Financial, Household, Personal and General. The chart which follows provides an outline of some typical file groupings to give you an idea of how a categorized system can work.

Notice on the chart the files are in alphabetical order within the categories. Bear in mind that these are just examples of file categories and names; you and your mate may need additional or different ones.

Depending on how your mind works, a categorized, alphabetized system can be much easier to use than a non-categorized one. Think about how supermarkets and department stores are set up: products are categorized together based on similarity. How long do you think it would take you to shop if merchandise was alphabetized instead of categorized?! Grouping "like items" together is a basic principle of organization as well as a human trait—even babies, after all, can categorize by color and shape. But if you've always used an A-to-Z system successfully, there's probably no need to switch over unless your mate will be in charge of all the household filing and he or she prefers categorizing.

EQUIPMENT AND SUPPLIES

If you and your mate do decide to use a categorized system, you have the added option of color-coding. This means that you can choose a different color to represent each category, using brightly colored file folders or file tabs. (These folders come in a rainbow of colors: red, blue, green, yellow, orange, purple, pink, aqua, black and gray.) Like anything else, there are both advantages and disadvantages to color-coding.

ADVANTAGES

- Substantially reduces misfiling.
- Simplifies file labels by reducing the number of words needed to identify files.
- Aesthetically pleasing.

DISADVANTAGES

- Costs more.
- Need to keep extra files and/or tabs on hand in different colors.
- Can become confusing if too many colors are used.

In a standard categorized (not color-coded) system, each file label must first state the name of the category, then the name of the actual file—"FINANCIAL: Banking," for example. In a color-coded system, a color represents a category (such as green for FINANCIAL); therefore, you're free to use the entire label for the name of the file. This usually makes for more readable, less cluttered-looking file labels—an important consideration in light of the fact that hard-to-read file labels can be a prime cause of marital anguish or at least misfiling.

Hanging file folders (made by Pendaflex, Datacom and Globe-Weis, among others) make files much more accessible and therefore easier to use. You can create

> *"Life is a crowded superhighway with bewildering cloverleaf exits on which a man is liable to find himself speeding back in the direction he came."*
> — PETER DE VRIES

subdivisions by using manila folders or matching colored interior files inside the hanging files. For example, if you have three types of insurance—Auto, Health and Homeowners—you'd label a hanging file "Insurance" and then label three interior folders with the individual types of insurance. (Labeling them with the names of specific insurance companies isn't a growth-oriented method because if you ever change companies you'll have to re-label files. But if you're used to doing it that way and your mate is comfortable with it, keep doing what works for you.)

Hanging files come with their own two-inch-wide plastic tabs (label-holders) which are either clear or colored, depending on the color of the files they go with. If you decide to color-code, you may want to get a few three-inch-wide tabs (purchased separately) to use on the first file in each category, to hold a label with the category name. This will ensure that neither of you will forget which color stands for which category.

Before you and your mate sit down to create the actual file labels, you'll need to decide which method to use: block-printing (all caps) by hand; typing; computer-generated; or labeling machine (such as described in the section on paper-flow systems, page 57). Hand-lettered, block-printed labels are the easiest to make and maintain if you can print legibly. As your needs change, you'll be able to quickly add or change labels just by picking up a pen. The other methods tend to be more time-consuming and therefore more likely to be postponed, although they do produce consistently clear labels.

You don't necessarily need to house your filing system in a file cabinet, nor do you need to keep all your files in one place. For example, important documents such as birth certificates, marriage license, passports, wills, and insurance policies should be kept in a fire-resistant file safe (this is different from a plain metal box—those melt). Sentry makes a good one which sells for about 50 dollars (see page 185). In the long run it's less expensive than renting a safe deposit box, and it's also a lot more accessible. However, a safe deposit box is a better place for negatives of cherished photos as well as all magnetic media such as audio- and video-tapes and computer disks, not to mention other meltable items like heirloom jewelry. For those objects, you can get super-heavy-duty fire-resistant safes, but they're a lot bulkier and usually quite expensive. (See list of "What Records to Keep and for How Long" on pages 180–182.)

You may also want to consider putting a small file holder (like the one described earlier for action-files) in the kitchen area. This idea might seem bizarre until you stop to think about all the different types of paper that tend to accumulate there: coupons, recipes, take-out menus, instructions for kitchen appliances, articles about stain removal and entertainment tips, emergency information, etc. Having a kitchen mini-file can save you time on a daily basis. The papers you want there will always be close at hand so you don't have to run into another room for them, and it will be easy to put them back in the right place when you're done with them. Your kitchen file can also help keep your counters and drawers free of paper clutter. And if you use colored files, it can be visually appealing too.

Another alternative or supplement to the common file cabinet is the rolling file cart (see page 185), which can fit under a table or counter and can be relocated easily. Because the top of the cart is unenclosed, the files are always accessible—a boon to highly visual people who don't like to bother with drawers (except for the lacy kind).

There's also a product called the Hang 'N File that makes use of wasted space on the back of a door (see page 185). It's designed to hold either legal or letter size hanging folders.

STORAGE OF SUPPLIES

Don't make the mistake of storing extra filing supplies (hanging files, interior folders, tabs and labels) in with your filing system. Not only will they take up valuable filing space, which is usually limited, but empty files give the illusion that you have more files in use than you actually do. This can make the system intimidating and confusing to use, especially for the mate who doesn't use it often. Also, it's easy when you're in a hurry to mistakenly stuff a piece of paper in an empty file located next to the one you intended to use. You or your mate may later waste several frustrating hours trying to locate that piece of paper. If you do have plenty of file space and prefer to store extra files in file drawers, isolate them in one drawer instead of mixing them throughout the system. They can also be stored horizontally in their original boxes or in regular drawers with other paper-type supplies.

 TIMELY TIPS

- Instructions and warranties come in a variety of shapes, sizes and thicknesses, and therefore can be awkward to file. Instead of stuffing them in folders and hoping you'll never need to look at them again (you will), you can organize them in loose-leaf binders paired with top-loading plastic sheet protectors and divider pockets. Some instruction pamphlets come already hole-punched; the sheet protectors only need to be used for the odd-sized ones as well as for the warranties and related receipts. The tabbed dividers can be labeled by category or by area (i.e., kitchen, garage, home office). There is also a product designed specifically for organizing instructions and warranties. Called the "Warranty/Instruction Organizer" (page 185), it has 12 see-through pockets and can be stored in a drawer, bookshelf or file.

- Recipes also work well in a loose-leaf binder with top-loading plastic sheet protectors. Since sheet protectors wipe clean, the recipes you actually use will remain unsoiled by the usual clinging globs and splatters of cooking ingredients. And because they're clear, they eliminate the need to recopy recipes torn out of magazines which are continued on the reverse side. (Of course, if you'd rather spend time copying those recipes onto index-style recipe cards instead of having a romantic moment with your mate, go right ahead.)

- If you like the idea of using loose-leaf binders for various "file-ables" but prefer to keep them with your files, a product called the hanging ring binder may be just the ticket. This is a binder designed to hang in a hanging file system. Some even have retractable hanger-tabs so that they can either hang or sit on a shelf or other flat surface.

• Other odd-sized or bulky materials such as greeting cards (to send) and maps can be filed in hanging box files (page 184), which have closed sides and wide, cardboard-reinforced bottoms to accommodate these types of papers. Or you may prefer to use specialty items such as a greeting card organizer (see page 185), or pamphlet files, which work well for map storage (see page 185).

• For short-term but paper-intensive projects such as planning a wedding, refinancing your home, applying for a second mortgage, or remodeling and redecorating, you need a system that can be tucked in a briefcase or under your arm. The Mead Classmate (page 185) is a spiral-bound set of four different-colored, two-pocket folders (a total of eight pockets). It was actually designed for students but works well for others—after all, we're all students of life. The Classmate enables you to easily group papers together that you don't want to hole-punch or that are different shapes and sizes. You can use removable adhesive-backed stickers to label the pockets according to the categories of paper you'll be encountering during the course of the project.

Examples:

Wedding. You may be collecting things like bids, brochures, business cards, contracts, receipts and even fabric samples in these categories: Caterers, Florists, Photographers, Musicians/DJ's, Video, Hotels, Gowns/Tuxes, Invitations.

   Refinancing/Second mortgage. The lenders will ask you for such documents as: Mortgage Payment Records; Pay stubs; Property Insurance; List of Liabilities; Tax Returns; Profit & Loss Statements (if self-employed); Appraisals; Improvements Records.

   Remodeling/Redecorating. You'll probably be collecting the same kinds of papers as described under "Wedding," only in the following types of categories: Painters; Tile; Carpet/Flooring; Window Treatments; Electricians; Landscapers; Furnishings; Lighting/Electrical.

5

More *Space* for Sex: Bedrooms, and Other Private Places

ou've just walked in the door after a long day at work. You're exhausted . . . but eagerly anticipating the romantic evening you have planned with your mate. All week you've looked forward to this—a leisurely dinner by candlelight; a bubble bath for two; a passionate night on those satin sheets you've been saving . . .

But wait! Where *are* those sheets anyway? And who left that disgusting bathtub ring that will probably have to be blasted off with a blowtorch? And why aren't there any matches for the candles?

In the mood for love? You've got to be kidding. At the moment, you'd just as soon wring your mate's neck as nibble on it.

BEDROOMS

YOUR OWN SANCTUARY

One place that clutter and disorganization can definitely dampen one's ardor is in the bedroom. It's not easy to feel romantic when you're surrounded by piles of dirty clothes, stacks of undone work from the office, and other annoying reminders of all that awaits you in the outside world.

Bedrooms are private areas and should serve as havens. They should be peaceful, pleasant places, not arenas for chaos and dispute. A couple should look forward to entering their bedroom, knowing it's a place where they can relax and be themselves.

That doesn't mean you have to spend large sums of money on fancy furnishings and lighting. It means you should work together to make your room a place where both of you feel welcome.

But not everyone agrees on what constitutes peaceful versus chaotic. Bill and Jean, a couple I once worked with, were experiencing tremendous marital strife—in part because Bill felt that Jean kept her side of the master bedroom cluttered with books, magazines and objects from her various collections. When I arrived to help them get organized, I didn't think it looked quite as bad as he described it. But what mattered was that Bill thought it was a mess, and therefore it was straining their relationship.

In the bedroom, as in other parts of the house, it's important for couples to be clear about what their individual housekeeping standards are. One person may not mind if the bed only gets made on weekends, while the other person fumes if that same bed isn't made up with precision so that a quarter can be bounced off the tightly tucked sheets and spread. Or maybe you disagree about clothes being left lying around the room. Some people just seem

> *"Then, the cool kindliness of sheets, that soon smooth away trouble; and the rough male kiss of blankets ..."*
> — RUPERT BROOKE

incapable of putting their clothes in hampers or back on hangers, while others are religious about folding or hanging and putting away each item as it is removed.

One woman I know claims, for example, that her beloved hubby lives life rather obliviously. If there were a dead animal in the middle of their bedroom floor he would probably just step over it day after day, she says, at least until it got really stinky. So, the state of the bedroom, or any other room in the house, doesn't really affect him.

MAKING IT RIGHT

Some couples appear to manage almost effortlessly to have picture-perfect bedrooms with coordinated curtains, covers and pillows and nary a perfume bottle or sneaker out of place. The rest of us, however, have to work at keeping things neat and orderly.

Whether you're starting from scratch in a brand new space or looking to revitalize your tired old bedroom, the same rule applies: Know your needs.

Here's a step-by-step way to figure out just what will work for you and your mate:

1. Step back and look at the room. Walk around it looking at the way the furniture is arranged and the way you have things stored. Check the color combinations and the pictures on the walls.

2. Make a list of specific points you like and don't like about the room (size, dimensions, color scheme, furnishings, layout, etc.). Get your mate to do the same.

3. Working together, decide what you would and could change about the room. Keep in mind your budget, how much time you actually spend in the room, and how long you plan on living in this particular house or apartment. Be candid about your feelings. If you're uncomfortable with the pink lace and frills your mate has used to decorate the bedspread and pillows, say so. If you're still using sheets his Aunt Mary gave you for a wedding gift, and you've always hated them, now's the time to purchase some new ones that you both like.

4. Working with one area of the room at a time, begin making the changes you discussed. Here's a list of things that, aside from your bed, you might consider for your bedroom area:

- Furnishings—nightstands or similar bedside storage; under-bed storage, either the kind on casters or the type that attaches to the bottom of the bed frame to make drawers; and lighting sources.

- An interim clothing area—something to hang clothes on—the ones that have been worn once but aren't ready for the wash. This might include door hinge hangers, hooks for the back of the door, or a free-standing valet-stand to hold coats and pants.

- A hamper or similar storage unit to hold dirty clothes prior to washing them. For those who can't ever seem to put things away, a rolling, three-part hamper can make life easier (see page 186). The three sections make it easy to sort clothes. If you place the hamper in a convenient place, your mate will have no excuse, either.

- An entertainment center might include TV, VCR and stereo system.

- Bureau and dressing table.

You'll be amazed at what a difference just minor changes can make in how you feel in your bedroom and in your relationship with each other. For example, finding the right texture of sheets can be important. Some people like a soft, warm flannel feel, while others prefer cool percale or the silky luxury of satin. Also, fragrances can be a point of friction. One partner may love sweet smells and think it's romantic to sprinkle the sheets with powder or perfume, while the other—who may never have spoken up before—finds this practice annoying and the strong smell overwhelming. It's good to get these things out in the open and discuss them.

IN EASY REACH

One thing that makes a bedroom more livable is having everything conveniently within reach. When you have a sneezing attack at 3 a.m. it's nice to not have to climb out of bed and pad to the bathroom to get a tissue. Likewise, during spontaneous intimate moments, who wants to call a stop action so he or she can run get

some "essentials"? A nightstand or headboard unit with cubbyholes or drawers works well for keeping these types of important
items handy.

Here's a brief list of things you might like to keep within easy
reach of your bed. You might be able to think of several more:

- Lamp or light switch
- Tissues
- Towels
- Personal items (e.g. massage oil, lubricants, contraceptives etc.)
- TV/VCR remote controls (Some relationship experts recommend having a
  TV in your bedroom, others are dead set against it. You can decide for
  yourselves what works for you.)
- CD or cassette player with CDs and cassettes
- Lingerie
- Reading material

ALL WORK AND NO PLAY DOES YOU KNOW WHAT

If you're looking for the perfect way to kill romance and intimacy,
put an office in your bedroom and keep it cluttered with visible reminders of all the work that awaits you there.

Seriously, if you must have an office in your bedroom—and
when space is limited it really is a valid option—put a decorative
screen between it and the bed. This can provide instant tranquility.
It's hard to relax and enjoy anything when stacks of work or unpaid
bills are staring you in the face. To find a screen that fits your
room decor and style, check various import stores and interior furnishings catalogs. You can also get an unfinished one and paint it
to look like a garden—or a neat room.

Also, draw a definite line between work time and home time.
If you have a home-based busi-
ness, for example, it's quite easy
to let your work take over your
entire life. You think to yourself
that you'll just spend a few min-

"Bed is the poor man's opera."
— *ITALIAN PROVERB*

utes working on Sunday morning and before you know it, Sunday night has arrived and you haven't set foot outside the house and you've hardly said hi to your mate (let alone participated in more intimate activities).

When possible, set yourself a regular work schedule and stick to it. And that means don't answer that business line when it rings on Sunday, even if it could be a new client. Whoever it is will probably leave a message or call back and you'll be more responsive if your private time hasn't been interrupted.

If your home office is strictly for paying bills and doing overflow work from the office, try to follow a similar routine. With your office work, judge how long it will take you to finish and schedule the time. But beware of doing too much at home. Relationships need work too, and if you're spending all your time on business your relationship is bound to suffer.

MAINTENANCE RULES & RITUALS

In the bedroom, as in every other room in a home, there are certain chores that must be done over and over again, ad nauseam, or at least ad tedium. In most bedrooms, for example, someone must regularly make the bed (daily?), change the bedding (weekly?), replace towels and personal items (as needed), pick up and put away anything left out (daily or twice a day?), empty wastebaskets (daily?) and dust, vacuum and clean (weekly?).

In many bedrooms, someone also regularly gathers and sorts laundry (weekly?), then after it's washed, folds it and puts it in drawers or closets. In some homes, there is also a mending basket where shirts missing buttons and skirts without hems bide their time until someone (perhaps a tailor) repairs them.

Making a ritual out of certain of these tasks can make them easier to complete and pos-

> "A coin ... or a collar button dropped in a bedroom will hide itself and be hard to find. A handkerchief in bed can't be found."
>
> — MARK TWAIN

> "I do all my writing in bed; everybody knows I do my best work there."
>
> — MAE WEST

sibly more enjoyable. Granted, some tasks are easier to ritualize than others. The daily grind of making the bed, for example, can be made easier by using a comforter and comforter cover (or duvet). Comforters are attractive, yet need not be tucked in, and a comforter cover can be removed and laundered much more easily than the comforter itself. The only ritual involved here may be the time of day you choose to make the bed. If you and your mate usually climb out of bed at the same time each day, it's easy for each of you to grab your side of the covers and spread them neatly. For mates who arise at different times in the morning, other arrangements could be made. Maybe you can take turns, one partner making the bed one week and the other the next. If one mate is dressed and out of the house before the other opens an eye, the task may fall to the late sleeper.

Hot Tip: Time yourself while making the bed; it shouldn't take longer than three minutes.

To create a maintenance ritual (or routine), certain guidelines must be agreed upon and established.

1. What is the purpose of the ritual?
2. What is the desired result?
3. What are the couple's agreed upon standards for this task or chore (especially for cleaning)?
4. Set a regular time of day and/or regular day of week to accomplish the task.
5. Mark it on your calendar with a reminder that can be moved from week to week (you can use different colored Post-it notes for different rituals or routines).
6. Agree on a set amount of time to finish the chore (a timer can be used).
7. Establish and provide the specific tools that will be needed.
8. Discuss specific methods to be used to complete the task. If you take turns doing a chore, don't complain about the way the other person does it.
9. If you wish, you may choose some special music to be played while you

work on the chore. If you or your mate is inspired by music, then by all means play it while you're doing maintenance chores. It can make the job go faster, or at least it will seem to.

10. What is the established reward for completing the task? (Maybe something with whipped cream!)

An example of a ritual might be the weekly changing of the bedclothes. Here's how it might work:

Purpose of task: To get dirty sheets off and clean ones on.

Desired result: Fresh, clean sheets to cuddle on that night.

Standards: Couple agrees that corners must be evenly tucked and bedspread spread without wrinkles. Perfection not required.

Set time: Once a week, on Saturday mornings while laundry is being done.

Tools needed: The only things needed to complete this task are clean linens. I suggest having at least two sets of sheets per bed, so that the set coming off the bed need not be laundered immediately.

Methods: Methods of bedmaking vary tremendously. Some people simply strip off spread, sheets, and pad and dump it all on the floor. Others carefully fold the dirty sheets and set them on a chair before proceeding to the next step. Find out if the method you use makes a difference. If it does, you should both try to use the agreed-upon method when doing the chore.

Reward: Rewards are personal choices, and each couple should establish their own. (See page 18 for a list of rewards or refer to your own list.)

BATHROOMS

Bathrooms, like bedrooms, are private areas. Also like bedrooms, the way they are set up and maintained can make a difference in how easy it is to share that space with someone. We've all heard the example of fights over toothpaste tops that get left off or toilet lids that get left up. Each of us has our own annoying habits, but

> *According to a recent Gallup survey, 60 percent of men admit they never clean the bathroom.*

if we start with a well-organized bathroom, those habits can be minimized, and sometimes avoided altogether.

Bathroom counters that look like department store cosmetic displays are hard to keep clean and can be frustrating to a partner who is trying to shave or wash his or her face. Likewise, it's unsettling at 6:30 a.m. to face a sink littered with shaving cream and ringed with tiny hairs. A little respect for one's partner goes a long way toward keeping the peace. So, have a place for all your stuff, and keep it there when it's not being used. And always clean up after yourself . . . you're not living with your mother anymore, you know.

Keeping things in their places sounds like a good idea, but most of us are long on possessions and short on storage space, especially in the bathroom. Part of the reason is what I call the "Discount Warehouse Syndrome." Many people have a tendency to buy more and more without considering where it's going to fit. At some point, you either have to stop buying or weed out what you have.

Everything in your bathroom should have a "home" and be easily accessible. Regularly used items should be close and easy to get to. Less frequently used things can be stored up high or down low. And don't be afraid to use your wall space. Many stick-on (adhesive-backed or magnetic) storage accessories are now available which can be used to keep things handy. For example, clear, stick-on "pockets" (see page 186) can be used to store scissors, combs, brushes and mirrors. Stick-on mini-shelves with built in drawers are also good for small grooming items (see page 186). These can be especially useful in small bathrooms that have no drawers. You can also buy stick-on wall dispensers for such things as shampoo, liquid soap and moisturizer (see page 186).

One bathroom area that always seems to act as a clutter magnet is the medicine cabinet. A good way to avoid this problem is to organize the cabinet using a device such as the Medicine Cabinet Organizer (see page 186), which has vertical compartments to help you categorize everything from medications to cosmetics to first-aid supplies. For the organizationally impaired mate, it might be helpful to label the sections to make it easier to put things back where they belong. A labeling machine (see page 184) can provide easy-to-read, adhesive-backed, waterproof labels.

Another good way to avoid clutter in the bathroom is to form the habit of discarding inefficient packaging from products that you buy and replacing it with reusable, convenient containers and dispensers. Rubbermaid, Sterilite and Tupperware all make handy, clear plastic canisters that can be used for a variety of products, including cotton balls and swabs, and personal hygiene products.

A major point to keep in mind when setting up a bathroom area, and when using it, is respect for the other person's space and property. If you're lucky enough to have two sinks in the bathroom, this is easier to do. But even if you must share a sink, try to designate a certain area of the bathroom and storage for each person. If possible, it's nice for each person to have his or her own towel rack, too.

THINGS TO DO
THAT MAKE YOUR MATE CRAZY
AND HOW TO AVOID THEM

1. *Use up all the toilet paper on the roll and don't replace it with a new roll.* To avoid this, keep a stash of extra rolls nearby or on the back of the commode.

2. *Every time you brush your teeth, leave globs of toothpaste in the sink and leave the cap wherever you set it down when you take it off.* Just take a minute when you're done to rinse down the sink . . . you'll both feel better. And with the variety of toothpaste dispensers available today no one needs to worry about the cap anymore. In fact, you can get toothpaste that comes with a flip-top cap so you don't even have to think about it.

3. *Whenever you bathe or wash your hands, use your mate's towel to dry off, then drop it on the floor when you're done.* Color-coded towels for each partner make it easy to identify which belongs to whom. Plus, keeping fresh towels as handy as possible encourages both parties to change to clean towels more frequently.

4. *Women—use your partner's razor to shave your legs. It really dulls the blade and makes shaving the face a real challenge the next time he does it.* Not only is this unsafe, but it might even be unsanitary. To avoid it, be sure that each person always has a supply of razors and blades on hand and in reach. That way borrowing isn't necessary.

Here's a list of items to keep in mind when setting up your bathroom for the utmost efficiency:

- Toiletries
- Cleaning products
- Hair care implements
- Personal hygiene products
- Towels/washcloths, etc.
- Reading material
- Paper products (toilet tissue, facial tissues)
- First-aid supplies
- Medicine cabinet stuff—pharmaceutical

CLOSETS AND OTHER BEDROOM STORAGE AREAS

When Vicki and Jake married they made the decision to live in the condo he owned. Since Vicki had been living with roommates for years she anticipated no problems finding places for all her possessions in the two-bedroom condo. But when it came down to unloading the boxes, she was in for a little surprise.

In the condo's large master bedroom there was a walk-in closet, an armoire with six large drawers and a nine-drawer chest. She thought it would be an easy matter to consolidate clothing

from at least five of the drawers
in the nine-drawer chest so that
she could use these drawers for
her things. Much to her surprise,
as she began looking through the
drawers, she didn't find a single
item of clothing; no socks, shirts
or skivvies. Instead she found:

> *"Lying in bed would be an alto-*
> *gether perfect experience if only*
> *one had a colored pencil long*
> *enough to draw on the ceiling."*
> — G. K. CHESTERTON

telephone wire, tools, old coins, nail clippers, extra telephones,
jewelry, and other odds and ends. Of all the nine drawers in the
chest, not a single one held any clothing.

Now, there's nothing to say you can't keep all your cords and
tools in a nice chest of drawers in the bedroom, but there are probably better places to put them in some other part of your house or
apartment. Vicki was finally able, through some judicious sorting,
to come up with four empty drawers for her own use. It took her
another five years to get Jake to clear the chest out completely and
use it for more traditional bedroom-type items.

HOME IS WHERE YOU HANG YOUR HAT/CAP/SCARF/BELT/TIE

One place we all try to hang everything is in the bedroom closet.
Not only do we hang things there, we also stack them, stash them
and compress them to make room for more stuff.

Take a quick look in your closet. Did you find items such as
purses you haven't carried in three years, snow boots that need repairing, and pants for your mate that haven't fit him in many
moons? Don't be depressed, many couples share this problem.
Closets are one area of the home where it's easy to let things collect unnoticed. Here are some actions you can take to change that.

THE IN/OUT INVENTORY RULE

This rule applies to other areas of your home as well as your closet
and bedroom. Simply put, it is this: Every time you bring an item
into the home, get rid of an item of equal size or shape. For exam-

> "Uneasy lies the head that eats crackers while in bed."
> — ANONYMOUS

ple, when you buy a new pair of shoes, go through and dig out a pair that hasn't been worn in ages and make a donation to the Salvation Army or other local charity. Or maybe your husband has just added a new sports cap to his collection. Since he won't part with another cap, look for some other item of clothing he no longer wears and see if he'll agree to let you put it in the giveaway pile.

Keep in mind when you're following the In/Out Inventory Rule that no one person's possessions are more important than another's. It may be hard to remember that when faced with a pair of plaid, polyester pants that should have been rag-bagged years ago, but are still your mate's favorite work pants. Just remember, you'd want the same respect paid to your favorite belongings.

SUBTRACT CLOTHES—ADD ROMANCE

If you and your mate tend to stockpile old, ill-fitting or unattractive clothes to wear just around the house, get rid of most of them and instead wear sexier things when you're at home together.

FIVE STEPS FOR ELIMINATING CLOSET CLUTTER

Most people dread cleaning out their closets, not so much because of the work involved but because they know they'll be forced to make some decisions about what to do with their "stuff." So, before you dig into the boots and cobwebs, take a look at these Five Steps for Eliminating Closet Clutter:

1. Set aside a specific block of *uninterrupted* time for your decluttering project. Make sure the phone, doorbell, TV, or other potential interruptions
   will not create distractions. Anywhere from one to three hours or more at
   a time is good, depending upon your energy level and the size of the project. Set a ticking, kitchen-type timer to keep you on track—it really
   helps to keep you focused. You'll also need to set aside subsequent "Errand Time" to help you deal with items you uncover that may need to be
   taken to the cleaners, recycler, tailor and so on.

2. If it's a large closet, or there is more than one, decide exactly which area
   or closet you're going to concentrate on for the allotted time period. Be
   realistic: If you have a lot of clutter, it's unlikely you'll be able to go
   through all of it in one session. Choose an attainable goal, one which will
   enable you to see results by the time your timer buzzes. For example, if
   you have lots of boxes and/or bags (or other types of containers) filled
   with "Miscellaneous," count them and decide how many you can tackle
   at a time.

3. Obtain six roomy boxes or plastic laundry baskets (square or rectangular)
   and label them (with stick-on labels) separately with the following categories: To Clean; Give Away/Sell; Recycle; Repair; Return; Keep. (Note:
   Different situations may need different category names, or different numbers or sizes of containers.) Also, have a good-sized wastebasket or trash
   pail (not just a bag) on hand.

4. Pick up only one item at a time, and decide which labeled container to
   put it in. Your goal should be to put as many things as possible in the
   wastebasket, "Give Away/Sell," and "Recycle" containers. Ask yourself,
   "How well could I live without this?" each time you find yourself waver-
   ing. Another indecision-buster is, "Is this item more trouble to keep than
   it's worth to me?"

   Items that do end up in the "Keep" box should be individually labeled
   (with removable stickers containing instructions such as "Kitchen—
   under sink" or "Office—bookcase"), unless you feel it is obvious where
   the item should be put.

5. When the labeled containers are full, you should distribute the contents
   as follows:

   To clean: Put washables in your laundry hamper; bag items to be dry-
   cleaned, label the bag "Dry Cleaning," put it in your car, and take it to
   the dry cleaners within 48 hours (or have someone take it for you).

   Give away/Sell: Use the same process described for "To Clean," modified
   for this purpose. Be honest about whether you will get around to having

a garage sale anytime in the near future; it may be ultimately more profitable for you to donate saleable items to a charity—especially if they'll haul the stuff away for you—and get a receipt for a tax write-off.

Recycle: Depending upon whether you have curbside recycling in your area or if you have to take the stuff to a recycling center (or call someone to pick it up), it can be as simple as sorting it into the curbside containers or as laborious as loading it into your vehicle and—as with the dry cleaning—getting it out within 48 hours.

Repair: Think about whether certain items are worth repairing or if it might be better to just donate them to charity and buy something more up-to-date. If you do decide on the repair option, then figure out how or where you're going to get the item(s) fixed; then plan to get it done within 48 hours.

Return: See "Repair"—same idea.

Keep: Carry the "Keep" box/basket from room to room, putting away items as you go. Always put things as near as possible to where they'll be used, and use hard-to-reach storage areas only for infrequently used items. If any drawers, shelves, etc. are already too full to add anything to them, ask yourself which items you can get rid of: the ones in the "Keep" basket, or some of the ones that are filling up the space where you want to put the items from the "Keep" basket? Something's got to go!

And if you're keeping too many things, using the favorite excuse of "I might need this some day," keep in mind that you can always get more stuff but you can never get more time. So stop wasting your valuable time by keeping too much stuff and use that time to have more fun with your honey.

BE CREATIVE IN YOUR SOLUTIONS TO STORAGE PROBLEMS

As you sort through your items to keep and look for places to put everything, be creative. First, you might sort items into five categories by frequency of usage:

1. At least daily—underwear, toothpaste/brush, hair dryer, etc.
2. At least weekly—favorite outfits, exercise wear and shoes
3. At most monthly—special occasion outfits, jewelry, certain shoes
4. Rarely, if ever—formal wear (i.e., tuxedos, costumes)
5. Seasonally—snowsuits, ski wear, gloves, hats, swimsuits.

As you decide where to keep these things, keep in mind the following general rules:

- The stuff you use the most often should be easiest to access.
- Keep infrequently used items in clear plastic containers (shoe boxes/sweater boxes) so you can see the contents and not forget what you have. If you don't use clear plastic, label everything clearly.
- Use a row or rows of hooks on the backs of doors or even on an open wall space to make it easy to hang things up. This is especially helpful for people who are inclined to leave clothes on the floor.
- Layer shallow baskets in deep drawers for underwear, socks and accessories. Frequently used items should be on the top layer.

 TIMELY TIPS

- If one partner is prone to leave stuff strewn around the room, or rooms, I suggest the following procedure:

  Have a basket handy in each room (size varies depending on situation). Establish a regular spot for it. Partners must agree that the designated "Clutter Police" person has permission at all times to sweep up/pick up all extraneous clutter and put it in the holding basket. At the end of each day, or when the basket is full, it must be cleared out by the clutter perpetrator, or contents will be tossed either into the trash or into a designated clutter area/pit.

  The good thing about this system is that it allows the person who prefers a clutter-free house to take some action while still respecting his or her partner's rights.

- Don't use the bed as a desk, hamper or dumping ground; it will start to become associated with clutter and chaos instead of romance and rest.

  I had a client who had gotten in the habit each morning of picking up all the "stuff to do" from the floor and heaping it on the bed—newspapers to read, bills to pay, clothes to mend, you name it. Each day she told herself that she would get everything done when she came home from work, but invariably she was too tired at the end of the day to do more than lie down so she'd dump everything back on the floor again. It got so she dreaded coming home to face "the stranger on her bed." Needless to say, her sex life wasn't exactly thriving—until she changed this dead-end habit.

- It's okay to have a phone in your bedroom, as long as you keep the ringer turned off (either all the time or before you go to bed). Also, unless you live in a studio apartment, if you have an answering machine try to keep it out of the bedroom. (Nothing can kill romance like hearing your mother's voice during an intimate moment.)

- Buy or make a "memory box" for storing any sentimental clutter you choose to keep: old valentines, special fortunes from fortune cookies, pebbles and shells from a particularly romantic beach vacation . . . anything that you or your sweetie can't bear to throw out and which doesn't really take up much room. Go through the contents together periodically—it should bring up happy memories and also help you weed out what is no longer as meaningful. And it will help cut down on clutter elsewhere too.

MORE TIME FOR SEX RULES TO GO TO BED BY

Take time to go to bed . . .

Earlier—Arrange with your mate to meet in bed a half hour earlier than usual. It will take some planning but the results are worth it.

Clean—Take a bath or shower (preferably together—to save water, of course) right before you jump in bed.

Comfortable—What you and your mate wear to bed—and what your bed wears too—should be whatever feels best to both of you. Whether it's lacy lingerie and satin sheets or plaid pajamas and flannel bedding, comfort in bed is necessary to romance.

Prepared—Stock your nightstands with everything you could possibly need or want during romantic interludes: contraceptives, lubricants, massage oil, towels, tissues, toys, snacks . . . anything you wouldn't want to have to look for later.

Happy—Set aside a few moments to clear your mind and, if you've had a disagreement with your mate, to clear the air. Count your blessings together and tell each other all the things you love about each other.

PART TWO

The Top 20
Organizing and
Time
Management
Challenges
Couples Face

*I*f you and your spouse really want to have more time for sex and other pleasures, you need to learn how to streamline and simplify certain areas of your life, specifically the areas that require regular maintenance and that can cause ongoing friction. Utilizing tools and methods that save time, energy and stress will make more time for sex a reality.

What follows are bite-sized breakdowns of the most time-consuming (and frustration-causing) ongoing chores and projects shared by the majority of couples, using real-life anecdotes to illustrate them—and real-life solutions to solve them. This section is designed to save you time by letting you skip right to the "challenges" that interest you the most.

THE TOP 20 ORGANIZING AND TIME MANAGEMENT CHALLENGES COUPLES FACE

1. Cleaning
2. Clutter Control
3. Cooking
4. Doing Dishes
5. Emergency and Disaster Preparedness
6. Entertaining
7. Errands
8. Grocery Shopping
9. Holidays and Special Events
10. Laundry
11. Other Shopping
12. Overnight Guests
13. Pet Care
14. Photo Maintenance
15. Recycling
16. Sports and Exercise
17. Taking Out the Trash
18. Travel Planning
19. Vehicle Maintenance
20. Yardwork

Cleaning

*J*ackie and Jim had barely returned from their honeymoon when she began thinking Divorce! The reason: A difference in cleaning standards. It wasn't quite that serious, but she did question his sanity when they began cleaning house one Saturday morning and he went and got the toilet bowl brush to scrub the kitchen sink. Luckily her shrieks stopped him in time. Jackie, who never ate a meal without first washing her hands twice, was horrified he would even consider doing such a thing and flabbergasted when he didn't understand what she was so upset about.

Renae faced a different problem when she first moved into her husband Wally's beach condo. He proudly boasted to her about his housekeeping prowess, claiming he was quite domestic. And it was true, the place was relatively uncluttered, with lots of clear space on cabinets and counters. A peek in the closet in the second bedroom, however, uncovered some definite packrat tendencies. Plus, when she started to take her first shower in what had been "his" bathroom, she was horrified to find a light layer of pink pre-

> "The only job where the work is steady but the pay isn't is housework."
>
> — ANONYMOUS

mildew covering the tiles on the stall floor. Wally thought he was a good housekeeper because he kept his place picked up and he always put things away, but he was actually spending very little time "cleaning." (When I read Wally this section to get his approval, he offered a charming defense. I quote—"I was actually a great housekeeper before I met and fell in love with Renae. After that I spent as much time with her as she would allow, so the house suffered.")

A difference in cleaning standards can be critical in a relationship. A floor that one person considers clean might make his or her mate run for a bucket and Lysol cleaner. Communicating your feelings about what you believe is clean is also important, but if you are the Felix member of an "Odd Couple," you may have to lower your standards just slightly if you wish to live in peace with your mate. Either that, or resign yourself to doing absolutely ALL the cleaning yourself.

THE CHALLENGE

Everyone (at least almost everyone) wants to live in a clean house, but . . . most of us don't really want to clean it. Coming home after a long, frustrating day at work and walking into a chaotic, cluttered living space only adds to your stress. Brushing your hair and putting on makeup in front of a grimy, water-spotted mirror at a grungy, hair-spattered sink can be downright depressing. But, so is spending every single Saturday morning or Sunday night scrubbing, vacuuming and polishing. There must be a compromise.

SOLUTIONS

Once you and your mate have resigned yourselves to the fact that **someone** has to keep the house clean, you have several options.

1. Find a way to stretch your budget so you can hire someone to come in on a regular basis and clean for you. (You might still have to do minor cleaning in between.) And if you're smart, you'll keep the place picked up. It's a waste of your housecleaner's time to pick up after you when he or she could be scrubbing and polishing. Plus, it's no fun spending Saturday night looking for things your help has put away when you could be enjoying each other's company.

2. If you opt to do the cleaning yourselves, create a list of chores to be done and decide between you who will do what and when (see sample, page 100).

3. Wait until the health department declares your home a disaster area, then move out.

Whatever option you and your partner choose, it's important to clearly communicate with each other (and your housecleaner, if you have one) what you expect the different areas to look like once they have been cleaned. This is critical if your cleaning standards are decidedly different. The following steps might help:

1. Sit down and draw up list of cleaning chores that must be done regularly.

2. Agree on who will do what when, and how often.

3. Determine the areas that must be cleaned: Bedrooms, Bathrooms, Living Room, Family Room, Dining Room, Kitchen, Garage, etc.

4. Discuss standards—what constitutes clean for these various areas of the home.

5. List the actual cleaning chores: Vacuuming; dusting; scrubbing floors, sinks, toilets, counters, etc.; polishing furniture.

Once you have decided as a couple what needs to be done and who will do it, don't constantly criticize the other person's work. If you are truly unhappy with the way he or she cleans a particular area, consider switching chores so that becomes your area.

A difference in standards isn't the only thing that can

> "A happy household is one where the wife helps her husband with the housework."
>
> — ANONYMOUS

> *"Keeping house is like threading beads on a string with no knot on the end."*
> — *ANONYMOUS*

cause friction in the house—a different focus can also wreak havoc. For example, Kathy had no complaints about the way Ed cleaned—when she could get him to actually clean. The day before Christmas Eve she was madly rushing around the house trying to get it clean for the ten family members coming to visit. In the kitchen, she still needed to polish the cabinets, clean the counters, scrub the sink and sweep and mop the floors. She asked Ed if he would mind pitching in and cleaning the kitchen while she moved on to other parts of the house. Two hours later he called her to come see the progress he had made, proudly showing off the fact that he had neatly organized every cabinet in the kitchen. Grateful though she was to have her kitchen in order, she was dismayed to find she still had at least an hour's worth of cleaning to do in there.

CLEANING CHORES

You and your mate can use this list to create your own schedule of chores to be done, listing who will do which chores and when they will be done.

KITCHEN

Daily
   Wash dishes
   Scrub sinks, counters, and stove top (includes polishing faucets)
   Take out trash

Semi-regularly
   Sweep floor
   Mop floor

Quasi-regularly
   Polish cabinet fronts
   Vacuum under refrigerator
   Clean out refrigerator/freezer
   Clean out and organize cabinets

BATHROOM(S)

Daily
  Clean up around sink after use

Regularly
  Wash mirror(s)
  Scrub sink and counter
  Scrub and disinfect tub/shower
  Scrub and disinfect toilet
  Take out trash

Semi-regularly
  Wash shower curtain/stall door to avoid mildew

As needed
  Replace caulking around sinks and tubs/showers

LIVING ROOM/FAMILY ROOM

Daily
  Pick up and put away daily clutter

Weekly
  Vacuum (carpet experts recommend more frequent vacuuming, but who has time?)
  Dust
  Wash windows

As needed
  Clean drapes, carpet and upholstery

BEDROOMS

Daily
  Pick up clutter

Regularly
  Vacuum
  Dust
  Take out trash
  Wash windows

Clutter Control

*O*ne person's clutter is another person's treasure; but for the purposes of this chapter, "clutter" will be considered anything that is left somewhere it doesn't belong: socks on the sofa, bath towels in the bedroom, computer disks on the kitchen counter. When one mate is in the habit of leaving a trail of flotsam and jetsam that the other mate feels compelled to pick up, disgruntlement and disagreements are sure to pop up.

Take the case of Larry and Leslie, a classic "Odd Couple"— Larry's the neatnik who finds joy in straightening towels and lining things up perfectly, while Leslie sails through life, leaving a trail of crumpled candy wrappers and rumpled clothes in her wake. Larry tried everything—begging, pleading, cajoling, wheedling and, finally, angry threats—to make Leslie "clean up her act." Nothing worked. Their sex life began to suffer because Larry's nagging tired both of them and helped maintain mutual feelings of frustration and impotence (in more ways than one).

Different organizational styles under one roof can cause tension in an otherwise happy relationship. Usually the partner with the more "relaxed" style is perceived by the neater mate to be a disorganized slob. The clutter that the sloppy one leaves behind is, to the "neatnik," like the proverbial red flag waved in front of a bull. It also serves as an ongoing, irritating reminder that the perpetrator cannot be controlled—an irksome and frustrating fact that is extremely difficult for the neater mate to accept.

Larry tried to simply ignore Leslie's "leavings," but that didn't work—his compulsion to pick up after her was just too strong. Leslie, on the other hand, really didn't care one way or the other whether Larry put away her stuff or left it alone as long as he didn't deliberately hide it or throw anything out without her knowledge. So Larry came to accept that he was cleaning up after Leslie for himself, not for her. Therefore, he had to let go of his annoyance at her.

This realization and subsequent acceptance (which took quite a bit of work on his part) freed him to enjoy the process of doing something for himself and, secondarily, for his wife. Because he'd always liked putting things away and making things neat it didn't really make sense for him to feel angry about doing it, once he allowed himself to accept that Leslie wasn't just leaving clutter around to provoke him. And Leslie actually started to make an effort to be less careless with her clutter when she began to feel that Larry wasn't treating her like an unruly child anymore.

In addition to dropping his nonproductive nagging tactics, Larry also resolved to relax some of his more compulsive neatening tendencies and focus instead on

> "It has long been an axiom of mine that the little things are infinitely the most important."
> — ARTHUR CONAN DOYLE

> *"Our life is frittered away by de-tail. . . . Simplify, simplify."*
> — *THOREAU*

streamlining his housekeeping habits to save time and stress. To that end, he adopted the following rules and tools:

1. Never spend more than five minutes per room each day on neatening, straightening or putting away. (Hey! That's a poem!) Use a kitchen timer (the kind that ticks loudly) to help adhere to this rule.

2. Picking up clutter should be limited to once a day; this eliminates the sensation that someone is "following along behind me," as Leslie described it. Resist the temptation to neaten things before the end of the day, except for special circumstances such as guests.

3. Make the process as efficient as possible by using a tote-basket with a handle (like the kind used in supermarkets; see page 186) to collect and redistribute all extraneous items. Otherwise there's a tendency to make extra trips from room to room, especially in a two-story home.

4. "Mystery items" (things that, to the neater mate, appear to be without any discernible use or value) should never be tossed without getting an okay from the mate to whom they belong. Agree on a holding place and a time limit for such items (generally a one-week maximum is reasonable); a final warning before tossing is a good idea.

5. Set aside a holding area or "pit." This could be a small room or a closet, or a corner of a room screened off with a folding partition, where the messier mate can be encouraged to leave things instead of sprinkling them throughout the home. If the clutter begins to ooze out of the designated area, the neater mate (by agreement) is allowed to intervene by either shoveling it back in or redistributing it. Throwing it out is only allowed with the permission of the owner of the clutter.

Note: If the messier mate has packrat tendencies, see Chapter Four for specific suggestions.

Cooking

*W*hen Jessie first met Andy, her entire cooking repertoire consisted of tuna melt sandwiches, chicken enchiladas and spaghetti. Needless to say, if the old saying had been correct and the route to his heart had been through his stomach, she'd probably still be single. Fortunately for her, he was raised by a mother who wasn't much of a cook either. He related horrid tales of his well-meaning mother cooking oatmeal before she left for work each morning, leaving him and his father to force down the cold, coagulated lumps when they ate breakfast an hour later. She was also known to cook hamburgers in a skillet on the stove, then let them sit in quickly clotting grease while she prepared the rest of the meal.

If those meals sound perfectly okay to you and your mate, cooking may not be an issue at your house. But, if you prefer your foods in a little more palatable state, read on.

THE CHALLENGE

If you and your mate are going to eat, someone's going to have to prepare the meals. Some folks skip breakfast. Others may get so busy they occasionally ignore lunch. But most of us traditionally eat three meals a day. Three meals a day, times seven days a week, times 52 weeks, translates to 1,092 meals a year. That's a lot of meal preparation. Fortunately for most of us, it rarely works out that way.

Many working couples eat lunch out during the week. Those who don't often pack a simple lunch or bring leftovers from last night's dinner. That leaves breakfast and dinner during the week and three meals a day on weekends. Breakfast these days is usually simple for our rush-rush society—a bowl of cold cereal and a cup of coffee. Or maybe you prefer toast, fruit or juice. That leaves dinner as the main meal . . . and someone has still got to plan it and prepare it.

SOLUTIONS

The solutions to the cooking challenge are almost as varied as the types of couples in the world. If one of you likes to cook, consider an arrangement where one cooks and the other cleans up. I've known several couples who manage quite well with this system.

If neither of you is crazy about time in the kitchen, but you like home-cooked meals, take turns preparing dinners and cleaning up. Or, more fun still, work together cooking and cleaning—a great time for catching up on each other's days.

The last choice, for those who can afford it, and to whom it appeals—eat out daily. But you still might like an occasional meal at home, if for no other reason than being able to eat in front of the TV together with your shoes off.

"I have measured out my life in coffee spoons."
— *T. S. ELIOT*

Whatever your preferred arrangement, remember it's okay to

give input when your partner is doing the cooking, but don't criticize or put down the way he or she does it. Too much of that and you'll end up doing the job yourself.

> *"Life is too short to stuff a mushroom."*
> — SHIRLEY CONRAN

One way many couples take some of the hassle out of meal preparation is careful planning. Some couples plan each day's meal a week in advance, then shop accordingly. That guarantees that you'll have the right ingredients on hand when you start the meal.

Another important rule in the More Time for Sex philosophy is to be flexible. Spontaneity in eating, like other areas of your life, is important. That may mean eating out now and then if the budget allows. Or how about ordering a pizza in and saving your energy for a little romance later in the evening?

One couple I know works together in the kitchen to prepare their special intimate meals at home. They take turns cooking, and the mate who is not cooking cleans the pots, pans and stove as soon as the cook is finished with them. The kitchen is clean by the time dinner is on the table. This way, when dinner is over, they put their dinner dishes in the dishwasher and can get on with their romantic evening without stopping to do the heavy cleaning in the kitchen.

OTHER IDEAS TO KEEP YOU COOKING

- Start a collection of simple, healthy recipes that you can throw together quickly. (Personally, I only save recipes that use five ingredients or less.)
- When you're preparing a favorite meal, double the recipe and freeze it for a future meal.
- Keep a list of suggestions for easy meals stuck to the refrigerator.
- Keep a small, spiral-bound notebook in the kitchen and use it to make a note of each night's dinner. It will help you avoid the "didn't-we-just-have-that-last-night" syndrome.

- Share a glass of wine with your mate as you work together to prepare your meals.
- Save time by buying the main entree for your meal (roasted chicken, an order of lasagna); then make some quick and easy side dishes and voilà—dinner.

Doing Dishes

*U*nless you and your mate order in or eat out every day and night (not necessarily a bad idea for some couples), washing dishes is inevitable. Of course, you can always use paper plates and plastic cups, but it's still likely that a certain percentage of your eating utensils will wind up in the sink awaiting a bath. Even if you have a dishwasher, dishes usually need to be rinsed and scraped and then loaded into the machine—all of which takes time.

Finding a way to share this thankless but necessary process in a way that works for both of you can be tricky.

Alex and Marilyn are a classic "Odd Couple." True to their stereotypes, Alex's tendency was to let dirty dishes pile up until there weren't any clean ones left before he'd get around to washing any; Marilyn's habit has always been to get the dishes done as soon as a meal is finished. They don't have a dishwasher because their kitchen is too small to accommodate one without sacrificing much-needed storage space. A dishpan full of soapy water is kept

> "The most popular after dinner speech that any mate can make is, 'I'll wash the dishes.'"
>
> — ANONYMOUS

in one side of the divided sink and Marilyn has asked Alex to at least put items to be cleaned in it instead of leaving them on the table where the scraps of food will congeal. But that's about as much as he'll do, most of the time.

Another bone of contention is that, according to Marilyn, when Alex does get around to washing any dishes, he often leaves what she describes as "globs of food" sticking to them. Alex, of course, thinks Marilyn is being "too picky." Marilyn ended up doing the dishes most of the time because she couldn't stand to see them sitting in the sink and she couldn't trust Alex to do them "right." This seemed to suit Alex just fine but Marilyn naturally found the distribution of labor unfair.

Although they use disposable plates and cups about 50 percent of the time, that still leaves enough dirty dishes (not to mention knives, forks, spoons, pots and pans) to create a simmering stew of resentment and irritation—hardly conducive to romance. A sticky situation—literally.

THE CHALLENGE

Conflicting styles and standards can make it difficult to agree on how often and how thoroughly the dishes should be washed. If one mate ends up unwillingly taking on the bulk of the chore on a regular basis, there's bound to be repercussions in other areas. ("Not tonight, dear ... I have a headache caused by DOING TOO MANY DISHES!")

SOLUTIONS

Examining the issue, Marilyn had to come to terms with the fact that the problem was basically hers because Alex really didn't perceive anything wrong with how—or how often—he did the dishes. So she came up with a solution that keeps them both happy: He uses a separate set of plain dishes—"the uglies," as she refers to them—and utensils. Her set—a flowered pattern—is stored separately; her cutlery pieces, which have pink handles to differentiate them from the ones that Alex uses, are kept in a separate drawer. She doesn't care if *his* dishes pile up (up to a point, anyway), or if he doesn't wash them thoroughly. And voilà—no more arguments about the dishes . . . and no more headaches!

> *"These I have loved: White plates and cups, clean—gleaming . . ."*
>
> — RUPERT BROOKE

OTHER SOLUTIONS/SUGGESTIONS

Set up your kitchen for maximum efficiency to take the pain out of clearing the table, washing dishes and utensils, drying them and putting them away. Get rid of or store gadgets that you rarely or never use, and keep "essentials" to a minimum and close at hand. If your kitchen drawers have become a jumble of strange, sharp objects that make putting away the cutlery a dangerous adventure, set a timer for 10 or 15 minutes per drawer and clear them out— you can even do this while talking on the phone.

There's nothing wrong with having a junk drawer as long as it really does contain only uncategorizable odds and ends. But if all your drawers have begun to resemble a bad night at Pic'n'Save, it's probably time to take action.

One of my workshop attendees once asked me, "How big should a junk drawer be?" I asked how big theirs was. "A whole room," came the reply.

THE RIGHT TOOLS

Having the right tools is crucial to the successful completion of any job, including dishwashing. If you and your mate are using the same smelly sponge you had last year, and your dish-drying rack

> "The best way to avoid dish-
> washing is to have your spouse
> eating out of your hand."
> — ANONYMOUS

has acquired a grubby patina of age and hard water deposits, it's time to splurge on some replacements. Splurge figuratively, that is—most things you'll need are relatively inexpensive.

Depending on how elaborate your meals are and where you actually dine in relation to where the meals are prepared, using a serving cart or trolley can save you steps and therefore time. It needn't be fancy. For example, a rolling storage cart with butcher block top and open-mesh drawers (see page 187) can do double duty when used as a serving and clearing cart. Of course, if the storage drawers bulge unattractively with "junk drawer" items, you may want to throw a small tablecloth over the cart before wheeling it out.

Store dishes, cutlery and other regularly used utensils in the cabinets and drawers closest to the sink or dishwasher; it will save time when putting things away. There are many excellent yet inexpensive drawer and cupboard organizers available that can help speed up the process even more.

It's a good idea to periodically re-evaluate the contents of your kitchen cupboards. Keep your dining accoutrements streamlined by eliminating extras and replacing pieces that are worn out, damaged or just plain unappealing.

There's a tendency for people to fill up all available space and then try to cram in even more. Ask yourselves how many place settings do you really need to have handy? If you rarely entertain at home and never serve tea, is it wise to have a teapot and 12 cup-and-saucer sets crowding your cabinets? You don't have to get rid of them if you don't want to, but at least box them up and store them out of the way somewhere else.

Nowadays it seems that mugs are breeding in cupboards at an alarming rate. They've become a popular gift item not just between casual friends during the holidays but also from companies trying to secure your business (these are usually imprinted with insignias or cryptic slogans). Unless the two of you have an inordinate fondness for mugs and unlimited space to store them, just keep your favorites and jettison the rest.

TOOLS FOR WASHING AND DRYING DISHES

Detergent	Dishpan
Dishtowels	Gloves
Dish-drying rack	Sponge/scrubber

TOOLS FOR CLEARING AND PUTTING AWAY

Serving cart/trolley	Drawer organizers
Cabinet organizers	

One nifty item that can save hands (and tempers) and which is actually useful for a variety of cleaning chores is the Super Dishwasher with Nylon Net (see page 187), a net-covered sponge on a long, hollow tube handle. The handle opens at the end so it can be filled with dishwashing detergent, which is dispensed through the sponge. If you, or your mate, prefer to protect hands by using rubber gloves while washing dishes, but hate the smell that they leave behind, try disposable plastic gloves; otherwise, fleece-lined rubber gloves (available at many supermarkets) aren't too bad.

Challenge Five

Emergency and Disaster Preparedness

*I*n the last few years, devastating floods, killer hurricanes, major earthquakes and horrendous snowstorms have struck different parts of the country. In many of these disasters, hundreds and even thousands of people were left homeless. Those whose homes survived the wind, shaking or flooding were often left without water, electricity and gas for several days.

Unlike some disasters, earthquakes come with no warning whatsoever. It's impossible to get prepared immediately before one strikes like you can if you live in an area affected by hurricanes or major snowstorms. But planning ahead can help you cope with many types of emergencies or disasters.

Karen and Ken almost learned this the hard way. During a major earthquake in Los Angeles, Karen was literally thrown out of their bed. With the floor heaving under her, she searched frantically for her glasses—the only pair she had. She couldn't find them, partly because she can't see a thing without them and partly because the room was shaking so much. Finally, the shaking stopped and her groping hands found her glasses. Fortunately, they weren't broken. The incident, however, made her and Ken (also a glasses-wearer) aware that they each really need to keep at

> *"Contraceptives should be used on all conceivable occasions."*
> — SPIKE MILLIGAN

least one extra pair of glasses in a safe place where they won't get broken, in the event of another earthquake or similar disaster.

While being prepared for a major catastrophe makes sense, it's also smart to think ahead about the minor emergencies many of us face. For example, broken pipes can cause flooding in your home, resulting in significant damage. When Bob and Sue lived in a condo, the unit above them flooded, causing water to seep into their carpets. No one was home in the upstairs unit, so it took a while to get the water shut off. Bob and Sue's carpets had to be taken up and professionally dried and treated, then stretched and replaced.

A winter snowstorm can also wreak havoc by knocking out electricity, meaning at the least no TV, and at the worst no heat. Plus, although disasters may not seem like the best time for romance, statistics have shown that more babies are conceived during power outages. So, if children aren't in your plans just yet, you'd better keep some contraceptives in your emergency kit.

THE CHALLENGE

The term "emergency" means an unexpected occurrence requiring immediate action. It needn't be a catastrophic event to have an impact on your life. Losing your electricity during the middle of getting ready for work one morning inconveniences you. Losing power and water for several days following an earthquake or a storm obviously causes much bigger problems. The challenge is to be prepared as best you can to face a wide range of emergencies.

SOLUTIONS

The best way to deal with any type of emergency is to plan ahead. It may sound time-consuming to put together an emergency packet from a lengthy list of items, but if there's ever a time when you need to not be wasting time, it's during a true emergency. Not only will prior planning save you time, you'll also be less likely to panic if you've thought about possible emergency situations ahead of time.

Sit down with your mate and discuss the different types of emergencies you might be faced with (fire, flood, snowstorm, hurricane, earthquake) and discuss what the consequences of those emergencies might be. Then make a list of all the tools, equipment, clothing, foods, and other items that you would need to see you through such emergencies. You'll find that in many cases these items overlap.

MAKING CONTACT AFTER A DISASTER

It's also a good idea to decide on an outside point of contact should you and your mate be apart when a disaster strikes. Following major emergencies, local phone lines are often completely tied up. Consider making a friend or relative who lives out of state your contact; you might offer to do the same for them. If disaster strikes, you may be able to let that person know where you are and what your condition is so that he or she can pass that information on to your mate when they get through. If your mate can do the same, you'll both be spared the agony of not knowing how the other one fared. This outside contact can also serve as an information pipeline to friends and family who live outside your area, letting them know how you and your mate are doing.

The following list, taken partially from an American Red Cross Family Disaster Plan and Personal Survival Guide, might help you in your preparations:

HOME EMERGENCY SUPPLIES

Quantities of emergency supplies should be adequate for at least 48 hours. (Some experts recommend 72 hours.) A two-week supply is recommended as a minimum reserve of water, food, medicine and other consumable items.

SURVIVAL

- Water—2 quarts to 1 gallon per person per day
- First-aid kit—ample and freshly stocked
- First-aid book—know how to use it
- Essential medication and glasses—as required
- Smoke detector
- Fire extinguisher—dry chemical, type ABC
- Flashlight—fresh and spare batteries and bulb*
- Escape ladder—for second story bedrooms
- Whistle—on your key chain
- Radio—portable, battery operated*
- Spare batteries
- Food—canned or pre-cooked and requiring minimum heat and water. Consider special diets, such as for infants or elderly.
- Can opener (non-electric)
- Food for pets
- Blankets—or sleeping bags
- Money
- Watch or clock—battery or spring wound

* Some stores have solar-powered flashlights and radios, so no batteries are required. Check survival stores and catalogues.

SAFETY

- Heavy shoes—for every family member
- Heavy gloves—for every person clearing debris
- Candles—do not use for indoor lighting following an earthquake, they can cause fires.
- Matches—dipped in wax and kept in waterproof container
- Clothes—complete change, kept dry
- Sharp knife or razor blades
- Garden hose—for siphoning and fire fighting
- Hat or cap—protection from sun, rain and cold

TOOLS

- Crescent wrench (for turning off gas main), axe, shovel, broom, screwdriver, pliers and hammer
- Coil of 1/2″ rope
- Coil of baling wire
- Plastic tape
- Pen and paper

SANITATION SUPPLIES

- Large plastic trash bags and cans (for trash, waste, and water)
- Hand soap and liquid detergent
- Toothpaste, toothbrush, deodorant and dentures.
- Personal hygiene supplies
- Infant supplies if needed
- Toilet paper
- Household bleach
- Newspaper—to wrap garbage and waste. Can also be used for warmth.

COOKING

- Barbecue (camp stove), fuel for cooking, pots and heavy duty aluminum foil

CAR MINI-SURVIVAL KIT

- Sturdy shoes and extra clothes (jeans, sweater)
- Local maps
- Bottled water
- First aid kit/book and essential medications
- Fire extinguisher, flares
- Flashlight—with spare batteries and bulbs*
- Tools—screwdriver, pliers, wire knife, short rubber hose (for siphoning)
- Nonperishable food—store in empty coffee cans
- Blanket or sleeping bag
- Sealable plastic bags, premoistened towelettes

Entertaining

When Vicki and Jake married, they decided to have a small family wedding and then throw a big country-and-western dance party/reception to celebrate. Neither of them had ever planned such a large party before, but they visited the discount warehouse and made guesstimates as to how much food and drink they would need.

The night of the party, everything was laid out, with munchies on the tables and drinks at the bar of the rented room. The large refrigerator in the kitchen was full of goodies to replenish the bowls. The evening went well and the guests and hosts had a great time. In fact, Vicki and Jake had so much fun dancing and visiting with friends and family that they forgot all about refilling the food dishes. As they cleaned up that

> *"Giving a party is like having a baby—its conception is more fun than its completion, and once you've begun it's impossible to stop."*
>
> — JAN STRUTHER

night they realized their mistake. In addition to carting home a trunkful of wedding gifts, they also had two pounds of popped popcorn and crackers, plus a month's supply of onion dip, cheddar cheese and various hors d'oeuvres.

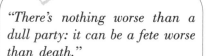

"There's nothing worse than a dull party: it can be a fete worse than death."
— ANONYMOUS

Although the party seemed to be a success, the host and hostess learned a lesson about entertaining: Someone has to be in charge of things *during* the party or event, not just before and after.

THE CHALLENGE

It's fun to socialize with friends at parties and special occasions. But sooner or later, you're going to have to be the one to play host or hostess. Doing so will take planning, scheduling, and a certain amount of poise when it comes time for the actual event.

There are several steps involved in successful entertaining. Someone (you, your mate, or hired help) must do each of the following:

1. Carefully *plan* the event, including schedules, guest lists, etc.
2. Shop for needed foods and supplies.
3. Clean the house before the party.
4. Clean the house after the party.
5. Act as host or hostess.

SOLUTIONS

If you both agree that entertaining is something that you want to do, it might be helpful to outline what needs to be done.

1. Planning: First, sit down together and come up with a mutual plan. What sort of party or event will it be? When will you have it? Will you serve food? If so, what kind and who will prepare it? If it's a more formal event, you might consider hiring a caterer. For informal get-togethers, a potluck is often fun. You can assign different dishes to different friends, so you are assured of a variety of choices.

2. *Duties:* It's always a good idea to make it perfectly clear who is responsible for what. Assign duties before the party—that way each partner knows his or her role. Then each of you can relax a little bit, knowing someone else is handling part of the hosting duties.

   The various duties might include: shopping, cleaning (before and after), taking the guests' wraps and purses as they arrive, insuring that every guest has met every other guest, preparing food, serving food, preparing and serving drinks, clearing away dishes, and washing dishes (after guests have departed).

3. *Party:* The most important part of entertaining, which often gets lost in the hustle and bustle—relax and have a good time. That's why you went to all this trouble in the first place.

Keep in mind when you're frantically running around trying to turn your house into something from the pages of *House Beautiful* that only the first few guests to arrive will even notice how spotless and shiny things are. After that, everyone's focus will be on the other guests, not on the house. So, get it reasonably clean and tidy, but don't be compulsive—save the wallpaper job for another weekend.

And remember to take time to give your mate a squeeze as you pass by on the way to refill the punch bowl.

Errands

*T*here are few things more frustrating than finding out your mate neglected to: a) pick up milk, b) make a bank deposit, c) drop off the video you watched last night, or d) all of the above. Like most things, errands are rarely noticed unless they don't get done. And the effects of un-run errands can be as minor as an extra $2.00 video rental charge or as teeth-grindingly ruinous as a batch of bounced checks.

When Gene asked Diane if she had time to take some bills to the post office for him, she said yes, and stuck them under the pile of letters she was planning to mail anyway. It wasn't until each of Gene's bills was returned for lack of postage that she realized why he had said "post office" and not "mail box." She apologized but pointed out that if he had been more specific about

> *"It is not true that life is one damn thing after another: it's one damn thing over and over."*
> — EDNA ST. VINCENT MILLAY

needing her to buy stamps she would have told him she didn't
have time that day anyway.

THE CHALLENGE

Running errands has become so time-consuming that errand service businesses are now quite commonplace. And considering the
range of errands most of us try to squeeze into our packed schedules on a weekly basis, hiring an errand-runner can be a relation-
ship-saver. The following list boggles the mind:

TYPICAL ERRANDS

STUFF TO TAKE SOMEWHERE

- Banking
- Things to mail
- Packages to be shipped
- Papers to photocopy
- Things to be passed along to friends, family, co-workers, etc. (including gifts)
- Books to return to library
- Purchases to return to stores (perishable and nonperishable)
- Clothes to be dry-cleaned
- Laundry to take to laundromat
- Clothes to be altered or repaired (tailor)
- Shoes to be repaired
- Other things to be repaired
- Film to be developed or duplicated
- Charity/second-hand store donations
- Recycling
- Video rentals to return

- Shopping (groceries, clothes, etc.)
- Stuff to be picked up (dry cleaning, repairs, etc.)
- Video rentals

SOLUTIONS

Whether or not you and your mate decide to get help with your errands or do them all unassisted, having an errands system can keep things running smoothly.

An errands system has two basic components: a designated area and a time limit. The designated area should be located as close as possible to the door which is used most often. (If you only have one door, life is simpler.) A small table or tiered rolling cart (see page 187) can be used to hold items that you're taking out or bringing in; small baskets or other containers sometimes work well in conjunction with the table. You might want to keep a plastic basket with handles nearby to carry the items to your car and on to their various destinations. A place by the door is also ideal to designate a "landing strip" for frequently used, and often misplaced, items such as keys, sunglasses and gloves. It's also handy to have a pen or pencil and paper or adhesive-backed notes there. Had Gene simply stuck a note saying "stamps needed" on top of the stack of bills he gave Diane, it might have saved them both a lot of grief.

If the two of you are holding your weekly planning sessions together (as described in Chapter One), then divvying up the errands should be part of that process. Some people like to do all their errands on the weekends; others prefer to work them in throughout the week, depending on their schedules. Whichever way works for you is fine. Either way, if you establish a mutually

> *"Life is a course that finally leaves you breathless from running around in circles trying to make ends meet."*
>
> — *ANONYMOUS*

agreed-upon time limit for any items that are placed in the errands system (24 hours? five days?), it's unlikely that the system will become a clutter pit. (Beware, too, the unfortunate tendency to simply dump stuff in the car in hopes that the errands will somehow run themselves.)

Be sure to take these factors into account while figuring out time limits and who will do what:

- How convenient is it for one or the other of you to run a particular errand?
- Does one of you have more time to run specific errands on a particular day?

Depending on how you like to do things, you may want to try setting aside time each week, or every other week, to run errands together and then have a casual date when the chores are done. Doing those everyday errands together is an opportunity to share hugs and titillating conversation as well as chores.

Grocery Shopping

*W*hen Nanci's husband Ben was a busy, harried law student and she was serving as the family's sole breadwinner, he tried to be as helpful as possible during the time available to him. He was always eager and willing to do the grocery shopping, but after several frustrating experiences, Nanci decided she'd rather just do it herself.

One day, however, she was particularly busy and asked Ben to just pick up a few simple items from the store. He gladly agreed, and listened patiently while she carefully went over the list with him. One of the most important items on the list was a jug of distilled water for their iron. She had important meetings the next day and wanted to press her blouse and suit that evening.

Ben returned from the store and proudly unloaded his bags, showing her how carefully he had followed her list. The last item he gleefully pulled from the bag was a gallon jug of distilled "vinegar," instead of the water she had requested.

* * *

> "The only food that never goes up in price is food for thought."
> — ANONYMOUS

Some people love to shop for groceries, others absolutely loathe it. Whichever category you and your mate fall into, once again, having a simple, flexible system will make the task much easier.

THE CHALLENGE

If you and your mate are going to eat, wash dishes, mop floors, and so on, someone's going to have to shop. To make that task as easy as possible, you need to know what to buy before you get to the store, which means making lists. So, separately or as a couple, you will need to make the list, buy the groceries, unload the groceries at home and find places to put everything. You might also need to spend some time budgeting the amount of money you want to spend.

SOLUTIONS

The first step toward fast and efficient grocery shopping is careful menu planning. Arrange to spend an hour or two each month planning various menus. Then, make a list of all the ingredients you'll need to prepare those meals. Do an inventory of your cupboards to see what you already have on hand. Then add the needed ingredients to your list. It's a good idea to do this part together: that way each person gets to choose some meals they like. If only one partner is willing to do the planning, it makes sense that the meals may reflect only that partner's taste.

Once you've planned your menus, there are numerous ways to make your grocery list. Some couples keep a piece of paper in the kitchen and as they run out of items or discover things they need, they add them to the list. Or you can buy preprinted sheets that list a variety of items most people purchase regularly. There are also products available such as the Jokari Shopping List Organizer (see page 186), which combines a preprinted list with room to add your individual choices.

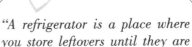

"A refrigerator is a place where you store leftovers until they are ready to be thrown out."

— *ANONYMOUS*

If both of you hate to grocery shop, you may need to do some negotiating and divvying up of the related chores. Vicki is one of those people who dreads a trip to the grocery store, less for the shopping than for the resulting task of hauling the bags home and finding shelf space for all the purchased items. She's been known to put off shopping until there's nothing to eat in the house but wilted lettuce and beef broth.

Jake, on the other hand, loves to shop for groceries, and doesn't mind all the related chores. But, without a detailed list, he often bought the wrong brands and sizes. Together they devised a solution. First, they created a computerized grocery list which includes all the food and sundries that they purchase regularly and semi-regularly. They even went so far as to organize the list based on the layout of their local grocery store. The list begins at the side of the store where the bakery is located, and works its way through the paper goods, frozen goods, dairy case, canned goods and fruit and produce. Over the years, the list has changed slightly as their tastes have changed. New items have been added and old ones deleted. The list hangs on the side of the refrigerator and anyone who finishes off an item or has a special request can write it down.

This system has made grocery shopping much easier. And, since all items are listed by brand name, and in some cases size, Jake can shop without fear of making a mistake (see a sample list on pages 130–131).

Another way to solve the grocery shopping dilemma is to split the chore into several smaller chores. For example, if one person makes the actual trip to the store, the other person might be responsible for unloading the bags and putting away the groceries. If you really, really hate the whole chore, you might strike a deal with your mate to trade for a chore that he or she loathes; or hire

someone to do it for both of you. Check with your local grocery
store and see if they offer a delivery service or look in the Yellow
Pages under "Shopping" or "Errands Services."

COUPONS

If you and your mate are coupon users, that adds an extra dimen-
sion to your grocery trips. See Chapter Four for specific suggestions. There is an item available that makes coupon cutting and
organizing easier (see page 63).

Although it's not always possible to plan our lives to the minute, it makes sense to plan a regular weekly grocery shopping trip
if you can. That way you can count on how long perishables such
as milk, bread and fresh fruit will last. It also helps with the menu
planning, making it possible to plan for such meals as "fresh" fish
on grocery shopping day, or similar dinners that require extremely
fresh ingredients.

VICKI AND JAKE'S
GROCERY LIST

BREAD
— Bohemian Hearth—Honey
  Wheatberry Bread
— Oat Fiber Bread
— Dinner Rolls/Italian Bread

SODAS
— PS Cola
— Mix

PET FOODS
— Nine Lives Packets
— Whiskas dry cat food

SUPPLIES—CLEANING, ETC.
— Dishwashing Liquid—Palmolive
— Sponge
— Liquid Soap refill

COFFEE, TEA, ETC.
— Orange Spice Tea
— Lemon Splash

CANNED—SOUPS
— Soup
— Tuna—white in water

FROZEN
__ Oat Bran Waffles
__ Popsicles
__ Juice
__ Frozen Dinners

SUNDRIES
__ Q-Tips
__ Shampoo—Perfect Choice
__ Hair Spray—Rave
__ Toothpaste
__ Other

SPICES/BAKING
__ Salt
__ Pepper
__ Other

CRACKERS/COOKIES
__ Soda Crackers
__ Cookies

CEREAL
__ Low Fat Granola
__ Life
__ Honey Nut Cheerios
__ Other

CANNED—OTHER
__ Tomatoes—recipe cut, 14 oz.
__ Spinach
__ Butter Beans
__ Lima Beans
__ Cut Green Beans
__ Ranch Style Beans
__ Beets
__ Beans
__ Spaghetti Sauce

DAIRY
__ Milk (nonfat—2 gals.)
__ Yogurt
__ Other

__ Eggs

SPECIAL FOODS & CONDIMENTS
__ Salsa—Herdez Mild
__ Paul Prudhomme Seasoning
__ Tartar Sauce—fat-free

DELI
__ Lunch Meat
__ String Cheese
__ Dill Pickles
__ Cheddar Cheese

FRUITS & VEGGIES
__ Bananas
__ Grapes
__ Melons
__ Pineapple
__ Apples—Granny Smith
__ Pears
__ Oranges
__ Potatoes
__ Cabbage
__ Lettuce
__ Green Onions
__ Bell Pepper
__ Carrots
__ Salad Mix
__ Other

Holidays and Special Events

*V*icki's dad was a wonderful man with a sometimes wicked sense of humor. He loved Christmas and everything it involved, from stringing lights to decorating the tree. One year, he decided to replace the traditional treetop angel with a bendable Santa Claus doll. The doll sat on the very top branch of the tree. When friends and family commented on this, her dad told them Mrs. Claus was feeling grumpy that year. One day Santa dragged in this huge tree, dropping needles and tracking dirt all across the floor. When he asked Mrs. Claus what he should do with the tree she couldn't control her response. So, that's where Santa sat for the rest of the season.

Many people feel just like Vicki's dad: They love all the hustle and bustle of preparing for holidays and special events. But there are others who feel more like Mrs. Claus did, grumpy and put upon. Whichever type you and your mate are, every holiday and major event will go more smoothly and be more enjoyable if you spend some time organizing and planning up front.

THE CHALLENGE

Every holiday or special event brings certain chores and challenges. The winter season holidays often mean decorating, shopping, wrapping, mailing cards and packages, baking, and for some people planning and preparing for guests and parties. Other holidays such as Thanksgiving, Easter and Passover often involve similar enjoyable but time-consuming effort. If you have relatives who usually prepare the holiday meal, you probably get off easy, maybe only having to bring a dessert or side dish. But if you're preparing the big meal yourselves, it's going to take lots of planning, organizing and cleaning, both before and after.

The importance of birthdays and anniversaries varies from couple to couple. For some, a simple celebration—maybe dinner out with a small gift—is all that's required to create happiness. Other people are used to a little bit more fanfare and won't settle for less than a party with friends and a mountain of gifts.

SOLUTIONS

As with so many other aspects of our lives, one thing that can make holidays and special events easier and more enjoyable is careful planning. Following are some general planning tips for holidays and special events:

- Make your plans early enough and flexible enough that you can adapt to any last minute changes that occur.

- Work with your partner on the plans so that each of you knows exactly what is happening and you both agree on the various parts of the plan.

- Keep an ongoing Holiday/Event To Do list and update it as necessary.

- For trip planning, see the section on Travel Planning (page 166) for ideas on packing.

- When planning special meals, keep it simple. When possible, involve some of your guests by letting them bring side dishes such as salads, vegetable dishes, rolls and desserts.

- When you can, clean up as you cook, washing pots, pans and utensils as you go. That way, when you're ready to sit down and eat you won't be staring at a messy counter.

- Plan ahead for dirty dishes and trash. Have a large trash can and trash bags easily accessible so a couple of people can quickly clean up after the meal.

- Don't forget about refrigerator and freezer space. If you're cooking for a large crowd, you may need more space than your refrigerator provides for storing ingredients before and leftovers after. Consider renting a refrigerator for a week to cover the gap.

- Try to plan parties in such a way as to minimize the after-party effort so that you can relax a little afterward instead of spending three days cleaning up.

- Keep decorations and other items that are for holidays and special events neatly organized and carefully stored. If any of these items are electrical, be sure they are in good repair before storing them. If they are inexpensive and you can't fix them yourself, get rid of them rather than storing them for another year.

- If your budget allows, make use of such services as caterers and cleaning crews.

Speaking of budgets, that's a critical part of planning for any event or holiday. Not only will budgeting save you money, it will also save you time. If it's a holiday that involves gift giving, decide before shopping just how much you can comfortably spend on gifts—and stick to it. For special events or holidays that involve travel, budget is also an important factor. Planning ahead may help you save money on air fares and hotels.

When planning your budget for certain holidays, be sure to include all the costs you'll be incurring. If, for example, you set aside money to spend on holidays each year, keep in mind you'll probably be spending money on things other than gifts. For instance, you may buy a cut tree to

> *"November runs into December, December runs into Christmas, and Christmas runs into money."*
> — ANONYMOUS

decorate and put in your home. And how about lights to decorate inside and out? You'll probably buy paper and ribbons to wrap the gifts you purchase. When those gifts are going to out-of-town friends and relatives, you'll

> *"Let's dance and sing and make good cheer, For Christmas comes but once a year."*
> — G. MACFARREN

also be paying for shipping. And if the holidays tend to bring out the generous side of your nature, you may be contributing more than usual to various charities. And don't forget that great new outfit you'll just have to have for the company party . . . and what about after-Christmas sales?

These days, Christmas isn't the only holiday that people go all out for. Stores now sell Easter decorations to put on little trees or bushes; strings of jack-o'-lantern lights and ceramic pumpkins; and of course scarecrows, witches and harvest wreaths are also popular in the fall. It may be fun decorating your home for the various seasons, but when the time comes to put everything away it can be a big headache.

So, before buying any more decorations for any holiday, decide into which closet or under which bed you're going to have to stuff it once the festivities are over. If you keep everything from each holiday together in one spot, it will make it much easier to decorate the next year. And don't forget the famous In/Out Inventory Rule—it applies doubly here. Every time you buy some new holiday knickknack or item, get rid of one of equal size.

There are several different products on the market that can make holiday chores easier. For example:

- Tucker and Rubbermaid both make large plastic tubs that are perfect for holding holiday decorations and accessories. You can even get them in red and green for your Christmas accessories (see page 187).

- Several different manufacturers make gift wrap organizers that let you keep wrapping paper, ribbon, tape and scissors all in one place (see page 187).

Laundry

*E*ven though, in this country, we no longer have to drag our laundry down to the river and beat it clean on the rocks, "doing the wash" is still a time-consuming, ongoing chore. Having access to a washing machine and a dryer doesn't eliminate the time and effort that must go into the chore: gathering and sorting the dirty laundry, pretreating stains, loading and unloading the machines, folding, hanging and putting things away—not to mention washing some items by hand, line-drying and ironing.

Like so many other household tasks, laundry is still considered "woman's work" by many men—and women. And like all such work, there's a tendency for most people to take for granted the time and effort of the person who performs the job regularly. Helen, a writer who worked at home, got fed up with her husband's lack of assistance and awareness when it came to getting the laundry done. Jason, a landscaper, had several irritating habits when it came to laundry. Not only did he tend to leave his dirty clothes on the bedroom floor, but he routinely forgot to remove tissues from his pockets, and his socks were always left inside out and full of earth and grass. Helen kept asking him to quit doing these things and Jason kept promising to try.

> *"What this country needs is a spot remover to remove the spots left by spot removers."*
>
> — ANONYMOUS

Things came to a head one evening when Helen opened the dryer and found that a paper towel (which had apparently been stuck in a pocket of Jason's jeans) had turned an entire load of laundry into what resembled a pile of dandruff. Helen loaded the pile into a basket, took it in to where Jason was lying on the couch watching TV, dumped it on the floor and jumped up and down on it with her dirty tennis shoes, screaming. Then she grabbed her purse and ran out of the house, slamming the door. Needless to say, Jason was startled.

When the dust (and dandruff) had settled, Helen returned to find a chastened Jason attempting to use a Dust-buster vacuum to rid the clothes of the paper residue.

THE CHALLENGE

Training others to change their laundry habits can be an ongoing challenge. Leaving clothes on the floor, not turning socks right side out and forgetting to empty pockets are signs of carelessness and not deliberate acts of hostility—although it may feel that way to the mate who keeps nagging.

SOLUTIONS

Helen explained to Jason that she really didn't mind doing the laundry, but she hated having to spend extra time literally sniffing out his clothes that were ready to be washed (which were invariably heaped together with his "worn once, still good" things), as well as searching pockets and shaking out socks. She also found it maddening that almost every time she did a load of wash and felt a fleeting sense of completion, she'd discover an errant pair of

> "*A pure heart is a good thing, and so is a clean shirt.*"
> — LICHTENBERG

filthy jeans or a grimy sweatshirt that Jason had thoughtlessly kicked behind a door or under the bed. They discussed various solutions. The possibility of Jason doing his own laundry was quickly discarded since his tendency was to wait until he had nothing left to wear before taking action, and Helen couldn't stand the idea of living with that. By focusing on streamlining the laundry process to save time and effort, they came up with some workable options that helped Jason become more cooperative as well.

Instead of trying to get Jason to use the bulky hamper in the bathroom, they found that a hanging hamper (page 187) in the bedroom (hung discreetly on the back of the bedroom door) was more accessible and therefore easier for him to remember to use. Helen also got one for herself which she hung on the back of the bathroom door; when the hampers are full, all she has to do is unhook them and carry them out to the laundry room—no more transferring from hamper to basket. Helen also created a sign that says "POCKETS? SOCKS?" with a funny face, which she attached to the front of Jason's hamper. With that reminder staring him in the face it's difficult for him to forget what he has to do.

Another product that can help cut down on time spent sorting laundry is the rolling divided hamper with attached lingerie bag (page 186). It provides three roomy sections for whites, darks, extra-dirty items or any three laundry categories you use most often, plus a large, zippered, mesh bag for delicates. Casters make it easy to roll from room to room. Zippered mesh bags in different sizes (page 187) also can be used for everything from delicate items such as pantyhose and lingerie to sweaters. (They're also useful for pairs of socks and gloves—no more mysterious disappearances.)

Having a laundry basket designated for clean clothes only is also a good idea.

Other Shopping

*W*hether it's clothes, supplies, gifts or gadgets, the same truth applies: If you need to buy something, you or your mate will probably have to go and get it. This act is called "shopping," and while for some people it's an enjoyable hobby, for others it's akin to Chinese water torture. Of course, emotions can fluctuate depending on the category of item that needs to be purchased. Sometimes the mate who would rather darn old socks than have to choose new ones is perfectly happy when let loose in a hardware store, while the spouse who can spend pleasurable hours at the accessories counter has no patience whatsoever in the electronics discount outlet. And shopping can become a real point of conflict between partners who feel equally pressed for time.

When Joan, a community college phys-ed instructor and part-time consultant, married Darryl, an entrepreneur with two businesses, she was horrified to discover that his mother still did all of his shopping for him—including underwear. Darryl, however, was perfectly satisfied with the arrangement, and it was with great re-

> "*Time is money, so when you go shopping take lots of time.*"
> — ANONYMOUS

luctance that he agreed to "fire" Mom's Shopping Service. Joan felt he should participate in the shopping process with her, since he wouldn't do it on his own, but she found that their busy sched-ules made this a seemingly insurmountable challenge. And since Darryl was relatively oblivious to the appearance of his wardrobe or their house, Joan found herself taking on the role previously filled by her mother-in-law the Shopping Fairy—and her resent-ment began to build.

THE CHALLENGE

Conflicting schedules can make it difficult for couples to share shopping duties. Too often, one mate gets stuck with the chore most of the time. And when the shopping entails purchasing clothes for the absent party, the amount of time spent can double because returns are inevitable.

SOLUTIONS

Joan hit upon a winning solution by accident while she and Darryl were vacationing in San Francisco. She'd taken to carrying with her a list of things he needed (everything from underwear to shoes) along with his sizes, so that whenever possible she could try to purchase something for him on her own. But being on vacation provided Joan with the rare opportunity of actually having Darryl with her most of the time. She took advantage of this and dragged him into a major department store with her. In less than an hour, with the assistance of some very knowledgeable sales associates, they were able to get him everything he needed to last him through the next year. Now Joan doesn't worry about shopping for Darryl— she just plans to do it while they're on vacation together twice a year. And although Darryl at first joked that he missed Mom's

Shopping Service, he now admits he prefers his current wardrobe. Especially the underwear.

"No man ever learns to shop properly: If he likes the first pair of shoes he tries on, he will buy them simply because they fit."

— ANONYMOUS

Another solution that is growing in popularity is the option of hiring a personal shopper. Some of the better department stores have begun to offer this service at no extra charge. There are also privately owned shopping services in many cities now (check your local Yellow Pages or ask around). Another possibility is to enlist the aid of a friend who likes to shop and whose taste you trust. Either offer to pay them to shop for you and/or your mate, or work out an exchange of services. Make sure to be clear about such arrangements or you may have some misunderstandings.

Shopping, whether it's for clothes or computers, doesn't have to be time-consuming drudgery. You and your mate can, with some creative planning, combine it with other things to do. For example, nowadays many shopping malls have cinemas and eateries along with boutiques and department stores. Why not make a date to meet your sweetie at the mall to spend a few hours of togetherness? (You don't have to be a teenager to do this.) Plan it so that you have about an hour between the time you finish dinner and when you need to be at the movie theater; this will ensure that the two of you have a useful chunk of time to share for whittling down that shopping list. If it's for longer than an hour, the mate who hates to shop will probably get edgy and irritable; don't push your luck.

If you are shopping with a mate who hates to shop but you finally get him to the mall, focus. Remember you are there to take advantage of this rare opportunity to save time and trouble, so don't get distracted by a fantastic sale in your favorite department.

Still another option is to shop by catalog. You can get virtually anything through catalogs these days (and that includes some things you and your mate might be too embarrassed to shop for in person). Some couples swear by catalog shopping; others hate to pay the shipping charges and are afraid they'll be disappointed in the merchandise. But if you shop with reputable catalog companies, you will save time in the long run. And that time can be spent snuggling with your honey instead of pounding the pavement.

Overnight Guests

*I*nviting guests to stay in your home can be delightful in principle but stressful in reality, especially if one member of a couple isn't a willing participant in the process. To some mates, being a gracious host or hostess means moving their legs when the guest wants to cross in front of their recliner; others think nothing less than recarpeting the guest room and providing gourmet meals is acceptable. Regardless of your style, in some situations problems can arise.

When Sylvia spontaneously offered to let a visiting friend stay with them for "a few days," she forgot to ask Ramon if it was okay with him. It turned out that he had never cared for this particular friend but had been too polite to say anything about it before. With no guest room—just a sofabed in the living room—the atmosphere became a little too close for comfort. Ramon ended

> *"In this cynical age nothing is sacred—except a guest towel."*
> — ANONYMOUS

> "Of all guests, the most unwelcome are those who try to make both weekends meet."
>
> — ANONYMOUS

up absenting himself from the house as much as possible, and it didn't help that Sylvia's friend managed to stretch the "few days" into almost a week. By the time she left, everyone was snapping at each other, and Sylvia ended up apologizing to Ramon for a lost week of connubial coziness.

THE CHALLENGE

Having guests stay with you and your mate for any period of time can have a negative effect on your relationship in general and your sex life in particular. The stress caused by reduced privacy and increased resentment can really take its toll on a couple's intimacy. In addition, when one mate makes a decision involving the other mate without consulting them, it shows a lack of respect that can, in turn, breed reduced trust between them.

The issue of house guests can cause these potential problem scenarios:

- Inviting guests without discussing it first with your mate.
- Inviting a guest whom your mate despises (friends or family).
- Not setting a time limit on the visit. (Remember Ben Franklin's apt observation that "Fish and visitors stink after three days.")
- Not having adequate space to comfortably share with a guest.
- Letting guests invite themselves to stay during an inconvenient time for you or your mate.
- Not being able to afford the added expense of feeding, driving and entertaining a guest.

SOLUTIONS

Each of the above points should be discussed with your mate before either of you even consider opening your hearth and home to guests. The consequences of not doing so can be potentially harmful to your relationship—not just with your beloved, but with your invited friends and family.

Ask yourselves, "What would be better for us as a couple?"

1. To have guests stay with us in our home
2. To put them up in a nearby hotel
3. To let them stay in our home and we'll go to a hotel! (may not be a realistic choice, but you could make it a romantic one)

If you choose the third option, and you're able to convince your guests that they're really not putting you out, this can be a relaxing interlude—a mini-vacation. Of course, this will work best if the timing is mutually convenient, and if there's an affordable hotel close by that both of you like. You don't have to spend a bundle on accommodations, since most cities now have some type of coupon book that can be purchased annually to obtain major discounts at restaurants, hotels and local attractions. And watch for off-season specials and promotional discounts. Whatever you do, try to get a room that's conducive to romance: a hot tub (or even just a big bathtub), a giant king-size bed, cable TV . . . You don't necessarily need a room with a view; they usually cost more, and wouldn't you really rather be looking at your sweetie anyway?

It can be fun to "vacation" in your own town and get to visit with your out-of-town guests when you want to. (For info and checklists on packing and travel preparations, see page 167.)

PREPARING FOR GUESTS

Preparing your home for guests, whether you intend to stay there with them or not, can be—depending on your situation—a matter of putting out some guest towels and fluffing up the pillows on the

"Visit, that ye be not visited."
— *DON HEROLD*

spare bed, or a mad scramble to clean up and stuff clutter anywhere it can be safely hidden. A Chore Poll conducted for *Special Report* magazine found some interesting statistics related to cleaning the house for company:

When men and women were asked "How long would it take to clean the house for a visit from your parents?" the average time specified by women was 5.4 hours, by men 3.5 hours. When asked "How long would it take to clean the house for a visit from your in-laws?" the answer was—women 6.1 hours and men 3.7 hours. And when asked "How long would it take to clean the house for a visit from out-of-town friends?"—women answered 9.9 hours and men answered 6.5 hours.

Of course, if you have a particularly messy room in your house, you can always throw everything in there; just be sure to keep the door locked, especially if you plan to leave your guests alone in the house.

Pet Care

*M*any couples, when they go out of town, have someone stay at or stop by their home to water plants, pick up newspapers and mail, and discourage thieves by making the place look lived in. However, when pets are involved it can be a lot trickier, as Ron and Susan learned.

They'd been planning their trip to Alabama for months and were pleased when Ron's 22-year-old niece, Rachel, offered to housesit and take care of the cat. They felt she was responsible and would respect their property—which she was and she did, up until one day before their return. Hurrying to make a date late that afternoon, Rachel rushed out of the house and slammed the door, leaving the house keys and the cat locked inside ... with no food and no litter box. Nobody else had a key to the house and she was forced to return to her

> *"Observe your dog: If he's fat, you're not getting enough exercise."*
>
> — *ANONYMOUS*

> *"The best thing about animals is that they don't talk much."*
> — THORNTON WILDER

own apartment and await Ron and Susan's return.

What a surprise—and what a smell—awaited Ron and Susan when they returned from their trip! Since then, they've decided maybe kennels are the answer.

THE CHALLENGE

Anyone who has ever owned a pet knows they are a big responsibility. Some, of course, require more care than others (snakes, for example, only eat every one to three weeks). The type of pet(s) you own dictates the type of care required. Cats and dogs are the most popular pets in this country, but birds and fish are also common. Some basic care that must be provided to pets includes the following:

- Providing them with fresh food and water as frequently as necessary. With cats and dogs that means every day.

- Making sure they get plenty of exercise and fresh air. If you own a home with a big yard you may not have to actually exercise your dog, but the attention you give them when you play fetch with them or run them around is worth almost more than the exercise.

- Cleaning up after them. With cats this might mean a litter box, which requires daily cleaning. Again, if you have a large yard for your dog, you're going to have a large area to clean up, unless you create a dog run or a fenced off area where the dog can be trained to relieve itself. If you live in an urban area and walk your dog down the street to do his business, please be courteous and clean up after him. There's no better way to make an enemy than to let your pet repeatedly use a neighbor's yard or front step for a toilet.

- Grooming them. Again, different pets require different amounts of grooming. At the least, however, you should probably brush your cat or dog regularly with the appropriate brush or comb.

- Giving them lots of affection and attention. Just feeding and watering your pet isn't enough. They like to be played with and talked to. This may become even more important if you work all day and the pet is left alone indoors.

- Providing care when you're away. When you must be away from home for any length of time, it's important to insure your pets are well taken care of in your absence, either at a kennel or by a friend or neighbor.

- Getting them regular shots and check-ups. Doing this can actually save you money in the long run. There are many illnesses that cats and dogs in particular are susceptible to, such as feline leukemia and rabies. Regular check-ups by a licensed vet will help you to keep your pet healthy. The vet can even let you know if your dog is overweight and needs to lose a pound or two.

As I said earlier, there's a lot involved in taking care of a pet. The question is, who's going to do these things?

SOLUTIONS

If one partner brings a pet or pets to the relationship, it's only fair that he or she should be responsible for the care of that pet. If the pet belongs to both of you, consider setting up a schedule to take turns with the pet care. If one person ends up being responsible for all the pet care, it can lead to resentment.

Providing affection for and attention to your pets is fun and easy; scooping poop and cleaning out the litter box are not. One solution is to train your pet to relieve itself in a certain area and/or at a certain time of day. Most cats and dogs are trainable. One couple I knew had a large pet collie that they trained to use a big wooden sandbox just as a cat might use a litter box. They still had to clean up after her, but at least it was all contained in one area.

For city dwellers who have to walk their dogs, the Walking a Pooch Pouch might make the process a little easier (see page 188); or create your own portable clean-up kit.

If you have a house cat, there's just no getting around the litter box issue. It must be cleaned out regularly. But today's "clumping" litter products actually do make it a little easier to deal with.

Photo Maintenance

*I*t starts innocently enough. First there are just a few envelopes of them—nothing to be concerned about, really, because they take up hardly any space. Then, as the envelopes increase in quantity and size, perhaps a "temporary" home for them is created in a shoe box or drawer. But as time goes by, they begin to multiply at an alarming rate, and then the overflow seems to take on a life of its own. (Too bad we're talking about photos here—how come it's never this way with dollars?!)

There never seems to be enough time to put all your photos into albums. And it often becomes worse once you and your beloved get married. Those hundreds of wonderful wedding photos usually end up languishing in boxes, baskets or baggies, just waiting for that proverbial rainy day when the two of you have nothing better to do than organize them. Of course that day never comes—unless you plan for it.

For Mike and Megan, photo clutter had become a growing source of aggravation and bickering. What seemed like countless photos, often along with their accompanying negatives, were stuffed in various places throughout their spacious home: a file drawer in their home office, a storage box in the bedroom, several stacking plastic bins in the

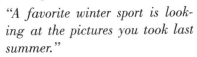

"A favorite winter sport is looking at the pictures you took last summer."

— ANONYMOUS

den, a lidded basket in the living room . . . these and more were bursting with pictures from every trip they'd ever taken together from their honeymoon onward. In addition, a number of stray rubber-banded bundles (usually photos of relatives and friends) had managed to escape into kitchen and bedroom drawers.

Both Megan and Mike were shutterbugs turned clutterbugs. They enjoyed actually taking pictures and were excited about seeing the results, but neither of them had ever gotten in the habit of doing something with the photos (aside from stuffing them away in a drawer) after the initial thrill of looking at them had faded. Because they had never discussed the topic there was no agreement on how the pictures should be organized or who should be responsible for which part of the process; consequently, each tended to blame the other for the ensuing chaos.

THE CHALLENGE

When each mate assumes that the other will handle a particular chore, problems—and clutter—can occur. And if neither party has a clue as to how to go about the task, it's easy to get stuck in an uncomfortable rut. Photo maintenance can be a particularly sticky area because there are no standard rules or guidelines—anything goes (or stays, as the case may be). Without an agreed-upon designated area or system for photo storage and a plan or process for maintaining it, the photographic piles will grow and grow—not a pretty picture.

SOLUTIONS

While visiting a friend's home one evening, Megan noticed several shelves containing pretty fabric-covered boxes stacked on top of each other. Slightly larger than shoeboxes, each one had a label in a little window on the front; most of the labels had dates on them, but some had other information as well. Curious, Megan asked about what the boxes contained and was enthralled when she heard that they were for photo storage. Her friend showed her that the boxes included tabbed dividers for separating and categorizing groups of pictures, and explained that she preferred the boxes to scrapbooks or albums because they were so much easier and less time-consuming to maintain. That was all Megan needed to hear before she was hooked on the idea; she found out how to purchase them by catalog (see page 188) and told Mike about it as soon as she got home. They agreed to order a few just to try them out. The system worked so well, they ended up ordering dozens. Of course, it took some time—several Saturdays, in fact—to actually get all the photos filed away, but Megan and Mike really got into it because they were delighted to finally have such a simple solution to what had seemed like an insurmountable problem.

Although the photos still aren't "perfectly organized," they are at least in some kind of order and, most important, they no longer create the sense of chaos that frustrated Mike and Megan. And they're determined not to let the problem recur: Now, whenever they get a roll of film developed, they sit down together at the kitchen table with the new photos and the photo file box at hand.

Other systems for organizing photos in a non-album format include photo flip-files and photo collage frames. Two catalogs, Exposures and Light Impressions (page 189), specialize in products for photo storage.

Another solution to the photo clutter dilemma is to find someone to either help you organize your pictures or do it for you. If you know of a person who seems to have a talent for putting together their own albums, talk with them about the possibility of hiring them to work with you on yours. Or check your local Yellow

Pages or classified ads, under Organizing or Personal Services, for services that might be available in your area. There's even a company that trains consultants (and their clients) nationwide to organize photo albums: Creative Memories (formerly Shoebox to Showcase).

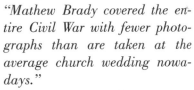

"Mathew Brady covered the entire Civil War with fewer photographs than are taken at the average church wedding nowadays."

— *ANONYMOUS*

It's also a good idea to store negatives from your favorite photos in a separate place such as a safe deposit box or at a relative's home, just in case of a disaster. Negatives take up much less space than prints, and you can always make more photos from them in case the prints are lost, damaged or destroyed. Remember, photos are often the first thing that survivors of fires and floods mention that they wish they'd been able to save.

However you and your mate decide to handle photo maintenance, keep in mind that the more pictures you take and keep, the more time and space you'll need to stay on top of them. But if all else fails, you can always sell your cameras and try to avoid photos altogether. After all, our ancestors managed to live just fine without them—and they certainly had a lot less clutter.

Recycling

*S*aving our earth by recycling newspapers, cans, bottles and plastic sounds like a noble plan. And each week, millions of conscientious Americans rinse out cans and bundle up newspapers, in an effort to do their part. But as noble and necessary as the recycling routine is, it can be a housekeeping nightmare for couples striving to keep their homes neat and clean.

Take newspapers, for example. For many couples, the day hasn't really started until they've had their first cup of coffee and read the morning paper. Some of these couples live in towns large enough to also have an afternoon paper. And if they live in a very large metropolitan area, they can probably also subscribe to a little regional paper to keep them updated on local news.

Ignoring for the moment the reality of finding the time to actually read all these papers, just think about how quickly this deluge of newsprint is going to build up. At the end of each week these couples are faced with large stacks of newspapers to toss out or recycle.

I once had a client who lived this experience to the fullest. When she first contacted me for help getting organized, she warned me that her house was probably the worst I had ever seen. Because I hear this frequently, I didn't

"Life could be worse: suppose the Sunday papers were published daily?"

— ANONYMOUS

think much about it. When I arrived to work with her, however, I discovered she hadn't been exaggerating one bit. The piles of newspapers, magazines, mail, photocopies, warranties and flyers were stacked to knee level all over the floor, throughout the whole house.

At the time, this woman was subscribing to three newspapers, dozens of magazines, and numerous newsletters, plus she belonged to several book clubs! The clutter had grown so bad that she couldn't stand to be in her own home, so she only went there to sleep.

Fearing she might impede my work, she asked if it was okay to leave while I worked on organizing her things. When she returned a couple of hours later, she was delighted. She could actually see the floor for the first time in years. And all I had done was sort the loose newspapers, stacking them in large laundry baskets. The unopened newspapers I stacked like cords of wood against a wall. I didn't have time to organize all the other papers, but I separated them as best I could.

I suggested that she should get rid of all the newspapers, but she was reluctant. The reason? "I haven't finished reading them." Dubiously eyeing the two huge baskets brimming with newspapers, I asked her how long she thought it would take to read just what was in those baskets. Heavily in denial, she replied, "At least a day."

Try as I might, I was unable to convince her to part with the papers. So I suggested that rather than keep them all around the house, she should rent a storage space somewhere and keep them there until she got around to reading them.

She took my advice and paid to store her piles of newspapers.

Believe it or not, a year or so later her storage unit was broken into and the newspapers were all stolen. (I can't figure it out either.) The manager of the storage company didn't offer much consolation—he suggested that maybe someone had done this woman a favor.

But all was not lost. She confessed to me that, though she had never told me this, she'd had so many newspapers she'd had to rent a second storage unit and the papers in that one were untouched. But, fearing further break-ins, she decided to move the papers home again. I did manage to convince her to stop subscribing to all the newspapers, so she is no longer adding to her piles.

Granted this is an extreme case of how newspapers can get out of control, but that doesn't stop me from using it periodically as an example to remind other clients to keep their newspapers moving out the door.

A WEEKLY RITUAL

Many years ago, I decided to stop subscribing to a daily newspaper because I hated the clutter it caused. Henry, however, enjoys his daily paper. So when we got married, I was once again faced with the task of dealing with piles of newsprint. Like my client, Henry doesn't always read the entire paper on the day it arrives. But he doesn't want it thrown out because he doesn't want to miss anything.

THE CHALLENGE

Piles of newspapers and other recyclables can create several problems. For starters, they take up space that could be used for something else. Also, when left undisturbed for a while, they can become a refuge for creepy crawlers such as earwigs and spiders. In addition, if left for longer periods of time papers begin to yellow and deteriorate, and can eventually become a real fire hazard.

Because Henry felt strongly about subscribing to and reading a daily paper, we devised a compromise. Newspapers would be stored in a designated area for up to one week; then they must be taken to the recycling bin. As a result of this solution Henry has developed a pleasant ritual for Wednesday nights, since Thursday is trash pick-up and curbside recycling day. He sits down with the week's papers to read and clip to his heart's content. I'm often out on Wednesday nights, so it's a quiet time for him to relax and enjoy—with no nagging. When he's done reading and clipping, the papers go out to the recycling bin and the clippings go into his office—otherwise known as "The Pit."

This solution takes care of the issue of being unable to "let go" of the unread papers. Plus, the process is made easier because we have a "mini-office" set up in a small basket on the dining-room table where Henry does his reading. The basket holds scissors, pen, pencils, Post-it flags, highlighter, paper clips, and a calculator.

If you are lucky enough to have curbside recycling service where you live, your job is much easier. If not, you've got to find a spot to gather all your papers (and other recyclables) until you take them to a recycling center. A large basket, crate or even box works well for this. Just be sure to drop them off on a regular basis. Once the piles get to a certain height, it seems to get harder and harder to make that trip.

Sports and Exercise

*P*aul and Lynn were excited about moving to Seattle from San Diego. They looked forward to the change in climate and the chance to meet new friends. It soon became apparent, however, that their new schedules didn't leave much time for the sort of exercise regimen they had been used to.

Lynn had been hired to open a new ambulatory surgery wing at a Seattle hospital, so she was spending long hours at work. Paul, an independent writer, was busy building a client base in the new town. Because Paul's schedule was more flexible, he was able to continue jogging, but Lynn was feeling frustrated at her lack of time for fitness. Finally, they came up with a plan that not only insures that they get some exercise, but also gives them some extra time together.

In the mornings, he drives her to work, stopping on the way

> *"Those who do not find time for exercise will have to find time for illness."*
>
> — *ANONYMOUS*

for a cup of coffee. It's a short drive to the hospital, but they enjoy the time to discuss the coming day. After dropping her off, he heads for the hospital pool to swim some laps. Several times a week when he picks her up, they meet at the hospital's fitness center and work out together before heading home.

They usually get home between 4:30 and 5, then take the dog out for a brisk walk. It's another chance to be together and discuss what their days have been like, while getting in some more exercise.

THE CHALLENGE

Like Lynn and Paul, the biggest problem most couples have with exercise and sports is finding the time for them. We all know by now that exercise is good for our bodies and minds, but when practiced correctly it can also improve our relationships, not to mention our love lives. Why? Because working up a sweat through some form of vigorous activity gives you a sort of inner glow and a feeling of peacefulness. This makes you easier to get along with and more attractive, which can't help but be beneficial to your relationships.

Other challenges couples face when it comes to sports and exercise include deciding what type of exercise is best for them and buying and maintaining any special clothing or equipment needed for those sports or exercises.

SOLUTIONS

The only way to find time to exercise either together or alone is to schedule it into your calendar(s) and stick to it. If Tuesdays and Thursdays are your nights to attend aerobic dance class, be firm about not accepting social invitations for those nights. If Saturday morning is the only time you and your mate can exercise together, then make that time sacred and don't let anyone talk you out of it.

Think of your exercise time as being just as important as

> "The human body is the baggage everyone carries through the voyage of life, and the more excess baggage one carries, the shorter the trip."
>
> — ANONYMOUS

work time and sleep time. Try to encourage each other to stick to a routine, but if occasionally one of you can't make it, don't use that as an excuse for the other to skip exercising that day.

When it comes to choosing a sport or type of exercise for you and your mate, be careful not to limit your options. You can get exercise doing any number of activities such as walking, running, dancing, playing tennis or racquetball, swimming, doing yardwork, and, of course, making love (although it's probably not fair to count that as exercise). Of all these, walking is the easiest and most accessible; it also provides an ongoing opportunity for couples to talk as they walk together.

Another thing to remember is keep it fun. Don't plan activities that are going to overstress you the first time out, so that you will be reluctant to do it again in a day or two. Keep it relaxed, and remember, moderation until you get in shape.

When you are planning activities, keep in mind the different ability and fitness levels of you and your mate. If, for instance, she's a star tennis player and you've just picked up a racket for the first time since your high school tennis class, it may make more sense for her to keep playing with partners at her own level for a while until you've learned enough to give her some challenge. Likewise, if you've been biking for ten years, don't make her first ride with you a grueling 50-miler, no matter what kind of shape she's in.

For some couples, competing against each other in a sport just isn't a good idea. Rather than sharing friendly, healthy competition, they end up being frustrated and holding a grudge. If you fall into that category, you can still get exercise with your mate, but try to limit it to noncompetitive activities like walking, running and bicycling.

CLOTHING AND EQUIPMENT

Another thing to keep in mind when choosing an activity is what type of clothing and equipment are involved, if any. Snow skiing is a favorite with many people, but it does require the proper equipment and clothing . . . and it's not an inexpensive sport. For running or walking, on the other hand, all you'll need is a good pair of shoes. I suggest making a list of all the various types of sports and exercise that interest you and your mate. Then next to each one, list the time commitment involved and the type of equipment needed to participate. From this, you can begin to narrow down your choices. (See sample list on page 162.)

Should you choose sports that require equipment, think about where you will store that equipment when it's not in use. With snow skiing, for example, unless you become real regulars on the slopes, you might consider renting most of your equipment for your ski trips. If cycling is more your speed, keep in mind you'll need a safe place to store your bicycle when you're not out riding. There are also certain paraphernalia that go with this sport, such as helmets, air pumps, patch kits, etc.

Finding room for sports and exercise equipment can be a real challenge, especially if your space is limited. Rowing machines, treadmills, stationary bikes, and other exercise equipment need to be kept set up, otherwise you'll never use them. Rackets, balls, gloves, hats and other sports accessories should also be kept accessible, for the same reason. It's too easy to rationalize reasons to avoid exercise; don't add misplaced gear to the list. You'll find it's easier to get motivated to play a few sets of tennis, for instance, if you don't have to search the house and the garage to find your racket and some balls.

If you really don't have the space to store a piece of equipment, resist the temptation to "buy it anyway." Your money would be better spent on a membership in a nearby health club that has a wide variety of exercise equipment to choose from.

Are you and your mate big sports enthusiasts? You might want to devote a whole closet to holding equipment and accessories. It can be quite convenient to keep all your equipment in one place; that way when you're packing for a trip or getting ready for an outing, everything is easy to get to.

It's also important to keep your exercise and sports equipment in good repair. Otherwise, you've got yourself another excuse for not partaking. And don't wait until the morning you've scheduled a racquetball game to check and see if you remembered to get your racket restrung.

For more major undertakings, such as the first ski trip of the year, it's wise to check out all your clothing and equipment a couple of weeks ahead. One way to do this is to lay out everything on the floor as if you were putting it on—pants, parka, boots, poles, skis, mittens, etc. Then check to make sure that any equipment is in good repair and ready to use. This will help you avoid the disappointment of reaching your destination only to find you've forgotten a key item. Those resort pro shops can be mighty expensive.

Even after you've laid out and checked over everything, it's a good idea to keep a checklist and check items off as you actually put them in the luggage or into the trunk of your car.

POTENTIAL SPORTS AND EXERCISE OPTIONS FOR COUPLES

Here's a list to get you started thinking about your sports and exercise choices.

COMPETITIVE

Bowling	Racquetball
Golf	Tennis

NONCOMPETITIVE

Bicycling	Skiing—snow or water
Hiking	Surfing
Jogging	Swimming
Rollerblading	Walking
Sailboarding	

Taking Out the Trash

*W*hether you throw it out, toss it, pitch it or give it the heave-ho, there's no getting around the fact that someone has to take out the trash. Yet getting rid of garbage is one of the least popular chores in any household. For couples, this simple but necessary act can cause complicated and unnecessary disagreements.

To Dana and Kevin the term "let's talk trash" had nothing to do with exchanging gossip. Approximately every other week Kevin would forget to put the trash out in time for the garbage service pickup; the result was smelly trash cans and a furious Dana—equally unpleasant. The final straw came when Dana claimed to have glimpsed a rat near one of the overflowing pails. After the screaming had subsided, Kevin agreed that he had to become more conscientious about the

> *"Marriage is not just spiritual communion and passionate embraces; marriage is also three-meals-a-day and taking out the trash."*
>
> — DR. JOYCE BROTHERS

> *"Familiar acts are beautiful through love."*
>
> — *SHELLEY*

chore, which was virtually the only household task he was expected to do. But he complained that the receptacles were heavy to lift and awkward to drag, and he was afraid of hurting his back in the process. Also, because their garbage disposal had been broken for years, he really hated having to deal with the kitchen trash.

THE CHALLENGE

Heavy trash cans filled with smelly garbage make an unpopular chore even less appealing. And procrastination makes this type of unpleasant task worse—the pails only get heavier and smellier as time goes by.

SOLUTIONS

There's more than one way to take out the trash so that it's not such a nasty process. Thanks to modern technology, some trash doesn't even have to be handled at all. Garbage disposals and trash compactors are now common conveniences in many households. Options on the low-tech side include: handy, under-the-kitchen-sink units such as the lidded Bag Holder (page 188) for potentially malodorous kitchen garbage; scented trash can liner-bags (in decorator colors, of course, and available at many supermarket chains) to class up your trash; and trash cans on wheels for easy maneuvering. There's even a special kind of wastebasket designed to utilize plastic grocery bags (see page 188).

After listening to Kevin's complaints, which were valid, Dana decided to take the initiative and arranged to have the garbage disposal repaired. That cut down on the smelliness but did little to change the heaviness, so they agreed to purchase wheeled receptacles. And when Kevin finally took Dana's suggestion to start marking "Garbage Out" in his planner every week, their trash trauma became a thing of the past. Now they laugh about the "rat ruckus"—especially since the "rat" turned out to be a stray kitten that they ended up adopting.

Taking out the trash often involves up to three steps: emptying wastebaskets and other receptacles into a large garbage bag, depositing the bag into a trash can or bin and—unless you live in an apartment or condo complex—carrying, dragging or rolling the container out to the street for pickup. Therefore, the overall chore can be divided up fairly easily between two people, with one handling the emptying and the other managing the depositing, carrying, dragging or rolling.

Travel Planning

*T*ravel planning—whether for honeymoon or holiday—can create almost more trouble than it's worth, or so it seems to some couples.

Long before our honeymoon, Henry and I had discovered that our travel styles were very different: easygoing Henry can sleep virtually anywhere while I need total quiet, a special pillow and ideal room temperature. He can happily wear the same pair of jeans for three days straight, while I have to change outfits at least once a day. Packing, to Henry, means grabbing whatever's handy and stuffing it in a gym bag about 20 minutes before departure; I, on the other hand, work from computerized checklists and obsessively pack and repack luggage, making sure *everything* is ready to go. Consequently, I ended up doing virtually all the planning and preparation for our bi-annual vacations. As our lives got busier, I found myself resenting what I perceived as the unfair division of labor. Things finally came to a head when I exploded over a minor problem and confessed to Henry that I was tired of doing all the travel planning.

Planning a vacation should be a joint effort. If one person winds up doing all the work, he or she can begin to feel more like a pack mule than a partner.

It doesn't have to be that way. If both of you are willing to be honest and realistic, and if you can learn to compromise as well as share the work, then vacations can be a wonderful time to refresh the romance in your relationship and catch up on the fun things you enjoy doing together (I'm sure you can think of at least one).

Start by making a list together of all the places you'd like to visit. There may be some destinations that only one of you would like to see—this is where the art of compromise comes in. If someone feels very strongly about visiting or avoiding a specific place, create a separate list called "Future Travel Compromises," put it aside (in a "Travel" file) and instead focus on the places you both would like to go.

The next step is to narrow down the list to the trips you'd actually be able to afford to go on within the next year or so. Use the Travel Budget Worksheet (see page 169) to help you be realistic. Be sure to take into account each other's travel styles: if your mate likes to camp out under the stars while your idea of roughing it is doing without room service, maybe you should see about renting or buying an RV or motor home or finding some other way to compromise.

Creating your own travel checklists—like other planning processes—can take time initially but save a lot of time over the

> *"One always needs a vacation, even if it's only to recover from the exhaustion of packing for it."*
> — *ANONYMOUS*

> "*The most important piece of luggage is and remains a joyful heart.*"
> — HERMANN LONS

years. Whether or not you have a trustworthy travel agent, a checklist of what you look for in accommodations can save you disappointment and frustration and can mean the difference between having a vacation that's a disaster or a delight.

Since quiet rooms are important to me, I made that point the focus of my Accommodations Checklist (see page 170). Many of the questions on the checklist were triggered by previous experiences. The form has thankfully prevented repeat occurrences.

Checklists for packing are great timesavers. In general, women's lists are longer than men's—mine is three pages while Henry's is half a page; see page 171. [*Editor's Note:* Although the authors offered to include Harriet's packing checklist here as a sample, we decided it would be of little value to most normal people.] It's helpful to categorize packing checklists (e.g., Toiletries, Outerwear, Camping Gear).

After I told Henry that what I particularly hated doing was making the calls to reserve hotel rooms and rental cars, he volunteered to take over those tasks. (It turned out he actually likes to choose the type of rental cars, something I always dreaded since I can't tell a Ford from a Ferrari.) And because Henry uses the checklists to ensure that every detail is covered, I don't feel the need to double-check and second-guess his decisions—all in all a much happier arrangement for both of us.

TRAVEL BUDGET WORKSHEET FOR TRIP TO _____
(Dates: _____)

EXPENSE CATEGORY   ESTIMATED COST IN U.S. $
                                    (INCL. TAX & SURCHARGES)

I. Transportation
  A. Airline
    One-way, per person $_____   Round trip $_____
    One-way for two   _____   Round trip _____
  B. Train
    One-way, per person   _____   Round trip _____
    One-way for two   _____   Round trip _____
  C. Car
    1. Rental charges
      Per day $_____
      Per week   _____
      Mileage/gas   _____
    2. Non-rental car (using own car)   _____
      Preparation/repairs   _____
      Gas
    3. Taxi or other ground transportation   _____
  D. Bus   _____
  E. Boat/ferry   _____
  F. Other   _____
II. Accommodations
  $_____ per night × _____ days =   _____
III. Meals
  $_____ per day × _____ days =   _____
IV. Entertainment/sightseeing
  $_____ per day × _____ days =   _____
V. Shopping/souvenirs/miscellaneous   _____

                                    TOTAL $_____

ACCOMMODATIONS CHECKLIST

Name of Hotel/Inn: _____ Date Called: _____
Phone Number: _____ City: _____
Name & title of person contacted: _____

A. How Noisy/Quiet Is It?   YES NO

1. Are pets allowed?   — —
2. Are infants/small children?   — —
3. Any construction planned?   — —
4. Other sources of noise (traffic, airport, entertainment, — —
   kitchen . . .)

B. Bathroom Facilities

1. Private bathroom?   — —
2. Bath & shower combination?   — —
3. Separate sink/counter areas? (toilet/tub in separate room) — —
4. Blow-dryer?   — —

C. General Room Info.

1. Non-smoking rooms available?   — —
2. Cottage (no shared walls?)   — —
3. If no cottage, single-story?   — —
4. If no single-story, top level?   — —
5. TV?   — —
6. VCR or in-house movie channel? (If VCR, what is charge for — —
   video rentals?)   ($____)
7. Clock/radio/alarm?   — —
8. Kitchen facilities?   — —
(Full __ Fridge __ Stove __)

D. General Hotel Info.

1. Heated pool?   — —
(Inside __ Outside __)
2. Dining room/coffee shop?   — —
(Hours: _____)
3. How old is hotel? _____
4. MC/VISA accepted?   — —
5. Deposit required: Amount: _____
6. Cancellation policy: _____
7. Reservation # _____

HENRY'S PACKING CHECKLIST

TRIP: _____
          (place)   (dates)

____ underwear   ____ socks   ____ T-shirts

____ jeans   ____ slacks   ____ shorts   ____ swim trunks

____ shirts   ____ pullover sweaters   ____ sweatshirts

____ belts   ____ tennis shoes   ____ shoes   ____ jacket

other: _____

_____

____ shaving kit   ____ aftershave/cologne   ____ deodorant

____ toothbrush   ____ toothpaste   ____ floss   ____ mouthwash

____ soap   ____ shampoo   ____ conditioner   ____ comb

____ brush

____ hand lotion   ____ First Aid (Bandaids, etc.)

____ watch   ____ travel alarm   ____ snack

other: _____

Vehicle Maintenance

*E*very family has stories they tell repeatedly about different family members. One story that Vicki heard early on in her marriage to Jake was about how conscientious his father was about taking care of the family cars.

Jake's dad was a school principal and school district administrator in rural Tennessee and his wife was a school teacher. Each morning, so the story goes, he would go out and check his car and his wife's car before they went their separate ways to work. First, he looked under the hood, checking the oil level as well as the levels of fluid in the radiator and the battery. Then he checked to make sure there was sufficient air in the tires.

Vicki found this story charming and expected a similar sort of devotion from Jake. Unfortunately, it wasn't a case of like father like son. Jake wasn't overly concerned about fluid levels and air pressure in the tires. He figured since there was a service station on almost every corner Vicki passed between home and work that, if she had car trouble, she'd be in better hands than his. He will occasionally take her car through the quick oil change station around the corner, and he's happy to fill the tank with gas if they happen to be together in her car when the gauge shows low.

"Some men take good care of a car; others treat it like one of the family."

— ANONYMOUS

Jake's not the only one with a more cavalier attitude toward car care these days. Times have definitely changed . . . and so have cars. We've gone from a full-service world to a self-serve world. If you don't know how to pump your own gas you're in trouble. It also helps to know how to check your oil, brake fluid and power steering fluid, not to mention tire pressure. However, cars are becoming more computerized and user-friendly, lights flash and beeps beep at you when certain parts need servicing. Some cars will even politely remind you to buckle your seat belt. Or, better yet, they'll do it for you.

THE CHALLENGE

Today's cars are expensive investments and they require basic maintenance to last. Someone must take responsibility for seeing that this maintenance gets done. That means one of you must do it—or hire someone to do it.

You can categorize what needs to be done into the following areas:

EXTERIOR

- Wash and wax (weekly or bi-weekly?)
- Tires—check pressure and tread wear

INTERIOR

- Clean and vacuum floors and upholstery
- Wash windows
- Dust and polish dash

- Organize glove compartment
- Pick up clutter from floors and seats

MOTOR/ENGINE

- Fill with gas
- Check fluid levels, etc.
- Take for regular tune-up
- Maintain, getting repairs done as needed

TRUNK

- Clean and vacuum
- Keep organized—tools, flares, etc.

SOLUTIONS

Discussing standards is important when it comes to car care. To some people, just having four wheels and a radio is good enough. Others may feel their cars are a reflection of them personally and they strive to keep their vehicles clean, shiny and well maintained. Stereotypically, it's the male who shows the most interest in car care, but that's not necessarily the way it is in all relationships. Discuss your feelings about your cars and their care and decide who will be responsible for taking care of each vehicle and/or area of the vehicles. With some couples it's easier for each person to be responsible for his or her own vehicle. Others interchange their vehicles regularly and so decide that one person should be responsible for both vehicles, or they might take turns.

> *"The goal of all inanimate objects is to resist man and ultimately to defeat him."*
> — RUSSELL BAKER

Whatever method you and your mate choose, it's essential to keep records on all tune-ups and repairs, especially when the vehicle is still under warranty. The better your records, the easier it will be to maintain your car, and to command a higher price for it when you sell it or trade it in. (See Chapter Four for information on setting up a Vehicle file.)

If neither of you is eager to take responsibility for car care, you might need to compromise. Take turns taking the car(s) in for servicing and repairs.

THE KEY TO STORING SPARE CAR KEYS

If you've never locked yourself out of your car by accident, you're probably in the minority. Most people who drive have had that wonderful experience at least once. And with the newer cars, breaking in a window to unlock the door can be next to impossible. The old coat hanger trick doesn't work well anymore. That's why products like the key holder that's disguised as a locking gas cap can be so useful. This device opens with a combination and cleverly conceals a spare key (see page 188).

Another option offered by many automobile clubs is an emergency key. Since it's made of plastic, it can only be used once, then it must be replaced. Contact your own automobile club for information on this product.

Yardwork

*W*orking in the yard and garden can be an enjoyable experience for couples who share a love of nature. Studies have shown that gardening also appears to reduce stress in many people. Then again, such chores as raking, fertilizing, mowing and weeding have been known to induce stress in couples who regard their yards as giant time-eaters.

Such was the case with Jan and Steve, a couple whose front and back yards began to lose their charm right around the time Steve was promoted to a position in his company that demanded longer hours. He had actually enjoyed working in the garden and was therefore reluctant to hire a gardener—he kept thinking that eventually he'd be able to manage the increased workload and handle the yardwork too. But as time passed and the garden looked more and more neglected, he was forced to admit that it was time to make a change.

Laura and Mark had a different problem: They had become addicted to upscale gardening catalogs and had managed to pur-

chase all kinds of fancy equipment—Swiss-made pruners, all
sorts of special sprayers, a state-
of-the-art mower—that began to
clutter up their garage. But they
rarely used any of the items because they had never found the
time to finish landscaping their yards, although they had purchased plenty of seeds and extra rich topsoil.

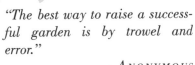

*"The best way to raise a success-
ful garden is by trowel and
error."*

— *ANONYMOUS*

THE CHALLENGE

Both planning a garden and maintaining it can be time-consuming
chores that generate an excess of tools, equipment and supplies.
And even if you enjoy gardening, it may not be possible for you to
spend as much time on it as you'd like, especially when your life
becomes more complicated.

SOLUTIONS

By doing some research (reading and taking a landscaping class
through a local community college), Jan discovered that certain
plants in their garden were creating a disproportionate amount of
work.

Replacing the "high-maintenance" plants with slow-growing
"low-maintenance" ones that were native to the area would cut
down on the amount of time needed to prune, trim, water and rake.
Steve reluctantly agreed to hire a landscaper to handle the re-
planting work, and when it was completed, he found the garden
much more manageable. Using the landscaper for basically a one-
time job enabled Steve and Jan to keep a lid on both the time and
the expense of maintaining their yards.

When planning a garden, always try to think of what will save
you time in terms of maintenance. This doesn't mean you have to
cement over your yard and paint it green (although that is certainly
an option)—there are other, less drastic possibilities worth explor-

> "A garden is a thing of beauty
> and a job forever."
> — ANONYMOUS

ing. Plantings that act like pets (you have to keep feeding them and cleaning up their droppings) should be avoided or kept to a minimum; it's wiser to invest in slow-growing plants that may only need fertilizing and trimming once a year instead of monthly. Find a nursery you like and don't be afraid to ask lots of questions; it will save you time in the long run.

Laura and Mark found this to be true when they finally decided to break down and get some advice on how to proceed with their garden planning and planting. They met a very knowledgeable nursery worker who was able to teach them some basics and help them make some time-saving choices. (Of course, when they found out that it wasn't necessary to spend more than $12 for decent pruners, they were somewhat chagrined—having fallen for a pair of $80 ones from a specialty gardening catalog.)

When they eventually finished planting their garden (after many weekends), they decided to hire a gardener to handle the regular maintenance. Not only did it free up their weekends, it also freed up their garage when they sold most of the unnecessary equipment they had accumulated. (And they used the money for a romantic weekend at a bed-and-breakfast.)

Like housecleaning, gardening involves plenty of dirty work that can, for a relatively small amount of money, be delegated to someone else. Unless you or your mate actually find fulfillment and joy while mowing, edging, raking, and sweeping, try to budget your income to allow for hiring out this type of work. It's impossible to put a price on the time and energy you'll save.

Be sure to take advantage of the latest technology in irrigation and watering systems. It's hard for most couples to find time to water by hand on a regular basis; investing in an automatic sprinkler system, for example, will save you time and the possible expense of replacing a dead lawn.

Afterword

Making more time for sex and other pleasures goes beyond sharing chores and streamlining systems. It's a mindset, an attitude that creates a joyful awareness of ongoing opportunities for intimacy with your mate. Just by getting in the habit of saying no to more stuff and more unnecessary obligations, the two of you can multiply your moments of togetherness. By focusing your attention on what really counts—your mate—you'll enrich not only your relationship but your whole life.

Ideally, couples need three lives: One for him, one for her, and one for them together.

—*JACQUELINE BISSET*

Appendix

WHAT RECORDS TO KEEP AND FOR HOW LONG

(This is to be used as a guideline only. Please consult your legal counsel or tax advisor for professional advice.)

RECORD TYPE	HOW LONG TO KEEP IT
Automobile	
Accident	Until claims settled
Gas and parking	For tax deductions, 4 years
Insurance	Until policy expires/claims settled
Purchase	Until car is sold
Payments	Until car is sold
Registration	Until car is sold
Repairs	Until car is sold
Title	Until car is sold
Warranties	Warranty expiration or claims settled

Bank
ATM slips   Until confirmation statement
Check register   4 years
Checks   4 years, longer if tax related
Checking statements   7 years
Deposit slips   Until confirmation statement
Passbook   Until account is closed
Savings: statement   Until account is closed

Bills
Charge account: statements   For tax purposes, 4 years
Credit voucher   Until confirmed on account statement
Installment payments   Until loan is repaid
Mortgages/Rent   Until home is sold or lease expires
Receipts/Bill stubs   For tax purposes, 4 years, longer if related to major purchase

Correspondence
Legal   Permanently
Personal   Optional

Dental/orthodontic
Bills   For tax purposes, 4 yrs. or until claims settled
Clinical   Permanent

Employment records
Contracts   Permanent
Correspondence   Permanent
Pay stubs   1 year
Recommendations   Permanent
W-2's   Permanent

Family records
Birth certificate   Permanent
Children's grades   Until graduation
Diploma   Permanent
Divorce settlement   Permanent
Jury service   Until next duty
Marriage certificate   Permanent
Military service   Permanent
Naturalization papers   Permanent
Passport   Until receipt of renewed passport
Pet papers   For life of pet

Social security   Permanent
Travel incentive award   Until expiration
Trust document   Until expiration or settlement of all claims
Will   Until settlement of all claims

Financial
Annuities   Until account is closed
Appraisal   Until sale
Brokerage account   Until account is closed
Certificate of deposit   Until account is closed
Disability insurance   Until cancelled or settlement of all claims
Life insurance   Permanent
Mutual funds   Until account is closed
Pensions/IRA/Keough   Until account is closed
Safety deposit box   Until account is closed
Stock certificates, bond   Until sale
Taxes
   Federal income tax   Permanent
   forms
   State income tax forms   Permanent

Household
Appraisal   Until house is sold
Closing documents   Permanent
Deed/Title   Until house is sold
Homeowner's insurance   Until expiration
Improvements   Until house is sold
Inventory of valuables   Permanent
Ownership manual   For life of appliance
Repairs   For tax purposes, 4 years
Property taxes   Until house is sold
Title insurance   Until house is sold
Warranties   Until expiration

Medical
Allergy   Permanent
Bills   For tax purposes, 4 years or until claim
                                     settled
Hospitalization   Permanent
Immunization schedule   Permanent
Medication   Permanent

RESOURCES LIST

PAGE   PRODUCT INFO

43   PRESTO LETTER OPENER
Keene Manufacturing Co.
(608) 257-2227

47   POST-IT MEMOBOARD
558
3M Commercial Office Supply Division
(800) 280-7402
(800) 362-3456

47   DECOFLEX
#23010–#23054 (9 colors)
Esselte Pendaflex/Oxford
(516) 873-3442

57   PENDAFLEX HANGING BOX FILES
#59202 2-in. width, letter size
#59203 3-in. width, letter size
#59302 2-in. width, legal size
#59303 3-in. width, legal size
Esselte Pendaflex
(516) 873-3442

59   ELECTRONIC LABELLING SYSTEM
Duratype 210
Kroy
(800) 776-KROY

59   AVERY PERSONAL LABEL PRINTER
#PLP5114 (IBM PC) #PLP5115 (MAC)
Paper Direct
(800) 272-7377

63   JOKARI COUPON ORGANIZER
#05043
Jokari
(800) 669-1718

PAGE   PRODUCT INFO

70   SENTRY FIRE-SAFE SECURITY FILE
      #1170
      (Available at most major office suppliers and some
          department stores.)

71   ROLLING FILE CART
      #85-797514
      Hold Everything Catalog
      (800) 421-2264

71   OVERDOOR HANGING FILE FOLDER RACK
      #669010
      Container Store Catalog
      (800) 733-3532

72   JOKARI WARRANTY/INSTRUCTION ORGANIZER
      #05050
      Jokari
      (800) 669-1718

73   GREETING CARD ORGANIZER
      #GCSB1
      Baldwin Cooke
      (708) 948-7600

73   PAMPHLET FILES
      #07222
      Fellowes Manufacturing Co.
      (708) 893-1600

73   MEAD CLASSMATE
      #33534
      The Mead Corp.
      (513) 865-6800

CATALOGS

Baldwin Cooke	(708) 948-7600
Colonial Garden Kitchens	(800) 245-3399
The Chef's Catalog	(800) 338-3232
The Container Store	(800) 733-3532
Exposures	(800) 222-4947
Hammacher Schlemmer	(800) 543-3366
Hold Everything	(800) 421-2264
Home Trends	(716) 254-6520
Light Impressions	(800) 828-6216
Lillian Vernon	(800) 285-5555
Paper Direct	(800) 272-7377
Reliable Home Office	(800) 621-4344
Starcrest of California	(909) 657-2793

RECOMMENDED READING

Byalick, Marcia and Saslow, Linda. *The Three-Career Couple.* 1993. Peterson's, Princeton, New Jersey.

Jhung, Paula. *Dirty Tricks for a Clean House.* 1995. Fireside, New York.

Kanarek, Lisa. *Organizing Your Home Office for Success.* 1993. Plume, New York.

Schlenger, Sunny and Roesch, Roberta. *How To Be Organized In Spite Of Yourself.* 1989. Signet, New York.

Silver, Susan. *Organized to Be The Best!* 1989, 1991 (rev.). Adams-Hall Publishing, Los Angeles.

Stoddard, Alexandra. *Living a Beautiful Life.* 1986. Avon Books, New York.

Stoddard, Alexandra. *Living Beautifully Together.* 1989. Doubleday, New York.

For Additional Help

Harriet Schechter helps couples, individuals and businesses get and stay organized through her customized consulting programs, seminars and workshops. She also offers training for people who are interested in becoming professional organizers.

For information about her consulting and presentation programs, please contact The Miracle Worker Organizing Service, 3368 Governor Drive, Suite F-199, San Diego, California, 92122; (619) 581-1241.

If you would like to receive information on how to become a professional organizer, send a stamped, self-addressed business envelope to the above address.